Catholicism
and Education

Catholicism and Education

John W. Donohue, S.J.

Harper & Row, Publishers
New York, Evanston, San Francisco, London

To The Memory of
My First Two Teachers

CATHOLICISM
AND EDUCATION
Copyright © 1973 **by John W. Donohue**

Standard Book Number: 06–041683–1

Library of Congress Catalog Card Number: 73–1035

Contents

v

Preface

This is a short book, but it touches on certain great themes to which many of us nowadays give some thought. Therefore, I have not been surprised to meet, at each turn and from every quarter, writers formulating, sometimes quite offhandedly, one or another of the ideas or impressions that drew my own attention as I worked on this topic. It might have been *The New Yorker*'s critic of rock records underscoring one contemporary mood with a deft clause: "A deepening sense of incipient disaster is making us turn inward. . . ." It might have been a theologian commenting on that familiar gap between belief and behavior that so embarrasses the effort to present Christian ideals persuasively. Or it might have been a sociologist ruefully noting that current reflections on Roman Catholicism are likely to be outdated before they can be published. And these convergences appeared only on the outer edges of the subject. There were many more substantial ones closer to the center, since any reflections about matters so vast and so much discussed as Catholicism and education must by now be more or less derivative. All these instances have pointed up the fact that a great deal in these pages is owed not just to books or persons but also to the common intellectual and emotional weather we are all experiencing today. For this reason it has not been possible to catalog my sources completely. When I have knowingly borrowed the insight or illustration of another, I have indicated that. But I am sure there are many debts of which I am hardly conscious or which are too general to be attached to the name of any one creditor. Yet these also I should like to acknowledge, if only in this indeterminate way. Finally, I owe specific thanks to Francis P. Canavan, S.J., and Joseph V. Dolan, S.J., for their wise comments on the final draft of this material and to James M. Kenny, S.J., for providing copies of the typescript.

Vibrations from Vatican II

1

... We can speak of a new age in human history.

Vatican II
"The Church in the Modern World," n. 54

Late in the summer of 1962 I was asked to do a short book on Catholicism in education for a series dealing with some contemporary philosophies and their significance for educational practice. The invitation was gratifying but not enough to goad me into immediate action and, as things turned out, that was fortunate. If that little book had been produced on schedule, it would have been out of date the moment it appeared. Moreover, it would have seemed that the author was embarrassingly unaware of this condition. To be dated is no great crime, but not to know it is no great credit either. Nowadays, if we talk about the problems of our civilization and the educational crises these create, we can hardly hope to escape rapid obsolescence as the problems themselves multiply and assume new and unexpected forms. But we should at least indicate that we recognize the plainly inevitable; and it has been precisely the years since 1962 that have forcefully taught such recognition to everyone interested in Catholic education.

It will be recalled that the Second Vatican Council was meeting for the first time in the fall of 1962 and was to hold its next sessions in the three following autumns. It is fair to say that the council did not so much create as manifest the arrival of a new era. On the last working day of their last session, the two thousand bishops who had come together promulgated their longest document. In it they noted that they had been gathering at a moment when "the whole human family has reached an hour of supreme crisis in its advance toward maturity."[1] Because moments of crisis are usually moments of questioning, it is hardly surprising that, since the close

of the council, self-criticism and innovation have flourished re-
markably among Catholics everywhere and not least among
Catholic educators in the United States.

This has meant changes both for the schools and for the educational theory they are presumably following. To be sure, the fundamental purposes of Catholic education, which we want to identify
here, remain stable. Nevertheless, the formulations of these aims
and of the means for achieving them are much more tentative now
than a generation ago. Moreover, even if the times were tranquil,
any generalizations about the large and complex American Catholic
school system would have to be compounded of several elements:
historical and sociological as well as philosophical and theological.

For instance, the mere record of historical growth is phenomenon enough. When the first national census was taken in 1790,
there were in the newly constituted United States about 35,000
Catholics, amounting to less than 1 percent of the general population of nearly 4 million. A year later John Carroll, the first native
bishop, opened an academy that became Georgetown University,
today the oldest Catholic institution of higher learning in the
country. When the 1970 census was fixing the nation's population
at close to 203 million, the *Official Catholic Directory* for that year
indicated that some 23 percent of these Americans, about 48 million, considered themselves Catholics. The one diocese of 1790
had multiplied to 160. The Catholic community had also reached
a critical point after a century and a half of building up its elementary and secondary school systems, for in 1963 enrollments
had begun to decline as fierce financial pressures closed hundreds
of schools. Still, in 1970 there were 9,947 elementary schools
(almost all parochial) enrolling 3,665,370 children, as well as 2,082
secondary schools (diocesan, parochial, and independent) with
1,054,642 students. In addition, exclusive of seminaries, there were
292 colleges and universities with 384,526 students. The whole
establishment, running from nursery school to graduate seminar,
was staffed by 199,468 full-time faculty members, including 85,616
sisters. In the elementary schools sisters still outnumbered lay
teachers by perhaps two to one, but in the college and universities
the lay faculty was a large majority and included a good many
men and women who were not Catholics.

If historians are needed to tell the story of the origins and
progress of these schools, sociologists must help us appreciate
their manifold variety and distinctive features and burdens. For
Catholic education ranges from country schools in the Dakotas,
taught by two or three sisters, to schools in Harlem enrolling as
many Protestants as Catholics; from riding classes in exclusive

boarding schools to complex urban universities with multimillion dollar plants (and enormous fiscal headaches), professional schools, and cosmopolitan pluralistic faculties.

There are three large questions, or complexes of questions, that might be asked either about the system as a whole or about any single institution within it. How can we solve those two perennial practical problems of financing Catholic schools and maintaining or improving their quality? What do the principles of a reasonable philosophy of education (that is, one legitimately derived from experience) require of these schools in the United States today? What do the principles of the Gospel require of Christian education in general and, therefore, of these schools in particular?

Since this book does not try to answer the first two questions at all, it does not summarize a complete theory of Catholic education (which would have to synthesize the conclusions of philosophy with those of Christian faith). Instead, these pages concentrate on that segment of the total theory which is drawn from the inspiration of the Gospel as understood in the tradition of Catholic Christianity, although from time to time we allude to the philosophical positions that complement the Gospel principles or are presumed by them. The next chapter examines some of the barriers confronting any attempt to speculate about Christian education; thereafter, our discussion deals chiefly with the aims that are set before that education by the Christian concept of man. Of course, this focus is not so very different from that of most philosophers of education. After all, Plato, Rousseau, and Dewey were mainly concerned with defining the nature of the good man and then determining the ends and means of education in light of this idea.

In line with this general approach, we try to indicate where the Gospel speaks about education and then to locate more exactly some of the goals it prescribes. But we have little to say about methods because in this area the Christian norm is largely negative. That is, it rules out cruel or dishonest, demeaning or coercive procedures; otherwise, it leaves to experience the devising of effective pedagogies. And so, perhaps surprisingly, we do not struggle with the formidable problems of religious instruction or character education, which are largely problems of action and method—of what is to be done. Within the basic Christian framework, the questions they pose require an empirical answer. For if there are a number of valid methodologies, Christianity will not demand one rather than another. What works best today, may be ineffective tomorrow. The high school religion texts that pioneered so strikingly yesterday are now remaindered. In her matchless biography of St. Thérèse of Lisieux, *The Hidden Face,* Ida Görres pointed out that the young Thérèse Martin was admirably educated in a tradition of firm discipline which is no longer attractive to most Catholics, although it had its strengths.

But even after our objectives here have been thus pared down, they remain daunting enough, partly because of the matters themselves and partly because of the character of our times. To begin with, an American who wants to talk about Catholicism and education has to be mindful of the complicated scene in his own country (even if he does not refer to it explicitly), because both halves of this general topic need certain specifications of time and place if they are to be handled at all. Such specificity requires an attempt to consider and enunciate, in terms of the facts and language of contemporary United States, principles which transcend that setting and rhetoric.

This is a troublesome necessity but not especially novel. It constrains anyone who proposes to comment either on Catholicism or on education, and thus it is not remarkable if it binds those who tackle both themes at once. For instance, in the theological encyclopedia, *Sacramentum Mundi,* the article on Christianity is by Karl Rahner, the most distinguished of living Catholic theologians. He remarked at the outset that the hazardous attempt to construct a brief synthesis of this kind can only have European and American civilizations in mind as audience. For our worldwide technology has not yet produced the common cultural outlook that would create a worldwide public for a text everywhere accessible. Thus other formulations must be devised for other cultures and, according to Vatican II, this is just what should be expected. For in the "Pastoral Constitution on the Church in the Modern World," promulgated December 7, 1965, the bishops observed that from the beginning of its history this Church has "learned to express the message of Christ with the help of the ideas and terminology of various peoples, and has tried to clarify it with the wisdom of the philosophers, too . . . thus each nation develops the ability to express Christ's message in its own way."[2]

The checks imposed by the particularities of time and place on the effort to devise general statements are felt still more acutely in the matter of education, for here we cannot even hope to address some unity called "Western civilization." The difference, let us say, between British and American education is considerable enough to oblige a writer to speak chiefly either to one or to the other—he cannot do both. In fact, even the once vigorous colonization of English educational ideals has broken down as the former colonies gain self-awareness. A black student at the University of the West Indies made this point less abstractly when he criticized Trinidad's school system. It turns out, he said, "excellent lawyers, orators and politicians, but no technical experts. For 100 years we have been brainwashed into being or trying to act like black Englishmen. But we are not Englishmen and never will be."[3]

Another reason for the difficulty of thinking or talking adequately about either Catholicism or education is that these themes require keeping simultaneously in focus the great visionary background of ideals and the harsh foreground in which the same ideals are necessarily specified and often betrayed. To take a single and obvious case, we must underscore the call to universal brother- hood which Christians received from their Lord: "This is my com- mandment: love one another, as I have loved you" (John 15:12).* At the same time, we must acknowledge the frequent and terrifying violations of this commandment throughout history.

Or again, we must firmly assent to all those vigorous tributes to education, from Heraclitus: "Education is a second sun to its possessors" to John F. Kennedy: "Education is the keystone in the arch of freedom and progress." At the same time, if we pass beyond these incontestable generalizations, we soon enough ap- preciate the crashing understatement of the Philadelphian who wrote in the *American Weekly Mercury* in 1735: "Education is in- deed a Word of a very large Extent. . . ." We cannot, for instance, overlook the sadness and boredom that fill so many hours of the school day and so many small heads. "If you worry too much, will you get sick?" "I don't like school." "Why do people die?" "Why don't married people be nice to each other?" asked elementary school children in Connecticut during the 1960s. And "What and who is God?" "How does He feel about love, marriage, sex?" asked the tenth-graders there.[4]

To ignore the foreground is to appear platitudinous. To ignore the background is to appear aimless. Reflections on Catholicism and education should be reasonably practical, while clearly grounded on the Christian message. At the same time, were there space for it all, the discussion itself ought to be inscribed at the heart of four concentric circles, to show an awareness of the world today, of the Church and its faith in that world, of contemporary United States with its strengths and limitations, and of the Ameri- can Catholic community and school within the United States. In any case, as the present essay asks about the universal implica- tions of Christianity for education, it must keep in mind the ques- tions and concerns of American Catholic schools. It must, in short have both a background and a foreground.

* All Biblical quotations are from the Jerusalem Bible.

Finally, two comments about terminology in these pages may also be in place. I am not, of course, supposing here that all Christians are Catholics, nor am I proposing a simple identification of Christianity with the Roman Catholic Church. On the other hand, I do myself profess that this Church is both a sign offered for the guidance of all men and a refusal, as Père de Lubac pointed out in his noble book, *Catholicism,* of all dichotomies. It affirms both nature *and* grace, faith *and* works, authority *and* liberty, the Bible *and* the Pope, rites *and* sacraments, as well as morals and the religion of the Spirit.

Hence, this Church is Catholic; that is to say, it is essentially universal and comprehensive. Thus I do not find the term *Catholic* displeasing, although I know some would avoid it either as having partisan overtones, as signifying a Counterreformation mentality that should be corrected, or simply as standing for something they dislike—one letter-writer to a Catholic publication declared genially that "Christian" and "Roman Catholic" are antithetical. In these pages, however (and this is the second point I would note), the terms *Christian* and *Catholic* are often used interchangeably, since I cherish both and would like to escape the monotony of using either exclusively. The context will indicate, I hope, when "Christian" or "Christianity" is designating beliefs and attitudes shared by Catholics and Protestants alike.

CHRISTIAN EDUCATIONAL THEORY AFTER VATICAN II

To think that the Second Vatican Council simply originated the current religious questions and inquiring spirit would be to demonstrate a spectacular ignorance of the history of the Catholic Church over the last four centuries. The council actually crystallized much that the Catholic community had experienced and learned about itself, particularly during the past hundred years or so. By 1870, for instance, the papacy had lost its Italian states and any real temporal power. But this was a blessing, for it freed the popes from the cares of petty monarchs and allowed them to concern themselves more effectively with the whole of the Church and mankind. Not long after, new movements in theology and biblical studies, in the practices of worship, and in sensitivity to the social implications of Christianity began to develop clarity and momentum. All these movements were promoted by one or more of the recent popes, and they all found voice in the conciliar sessions in St. Peter's. This meant the release of a number of powerful ideas that have fermented so strongly within Catholic life and education that it is still impossible to determine the full extent of their effects.

Although this chapter does not enlarge upon these pivotal ideas, one or two observations may serve to illustrate the council's significance for the themes of this book and to show why it is quoted or cited so often in the pages to follow. An overview of the council's documents reveals that they concentrate on the Church and the life of its members. Two aspects of that life are emphasized, and naturally enough, since they correspond to the two great commandments. On the one hand, the council hoping, as it said, "for a new surge of spiritual vitality," meditated on the relationship of men to God and its nourishment both by community worship and by individual inward growth of the contemplative spirit. On the other hand, the council urged Catholics to recognize that "the human family . . . comprises a single world community" and so to strive by themselves and in cooperation with all men to make that community truly human, a fellowship characterized by justice, mercy, and peace. These two calls—to interiority and to responsible work for the common human welfare—are the council's basic implications for Catholic education, and we have a good deal to say about these themes in later chapters.

In addition to these central motifs, other and more specific conciliar concepts are pertinent, not just for education generally considered but for schools in particular. These notions are not found in the more obvious places. The "Declaration on Christian Education," for example, is somewhat conventional. This is hardly surprising, since it treats principally of schooling, and schools, which are trying to communicate a way of life to the rising generation, are more preoccupied with conservation than with innovation. In the decrees on "Ecumenism," the "Apostolate of the Laity," and the "Church's Missionary Activity," as well as in the two great documents on the Church itself, however, there were at least four nuclear ideas that strongly appealed to American Catholic schools (partly, no doubt, because they articulated movements already under way). One of these ideas was the appreciative endorsement of what have come to be called secular or terrestrial values—the whole range of arts, sciences, technology, and civic enterprise involved in building civilization as both the support and the expression of a humane life. The other ideas were the firm emphases on the role and responsibility of the laity, not merely in human society as a whole but also within the Church; on freedom as the root of personal worth, dignity, and growth; and on community as a focal value flowing from the human family's oneness and common transtemporal destiny. This calls, in turn, for working toward the ideal of friendship and cooperation across all borders and at all levels, including the international.

These concepts reappear in one way or another, but we might point out now that the first two had been influencing American Catholic schools for some time prior to 1962. These schools had enlarged their appreciation of the secular dimension of their work because their own experience had taught them the wisdom neatly summed up by T. S. Eliot, when he noted that humanism without religion runs the risk of sterility, and religion without humanism runs the risk of vulgarity.[5] The schools set this insight within a theological framework that acknowledges for every Christian a twofold vocation in which the first aspect is ultimately ordered to the second. For Christians are summoned both to life in time and to life in the Age-to-Come; to the earth made by God and to union with God Himself. The corollary that the council's "Declaration on Christian Education" drew from this is that all children should be so educated as "to pace their development as Christians with their growth as citizens of the world."

During the 1960s it steadily became clearer that many segments of the Catholic school system in the United States were too large and complex for management by declining numbers of ecclesiastical personnel alone. One result was the expanding trend toward diocesan and parish school boards composed principally of parents. Another was the movement to transfer top responsibility for colleges and universities to boards of trustees on which laymen, including those of other faiths, were in the majority. The latter development might also be seen as an instance of that process of desacralization that has swelled constantly since the days of medieval Christendom and the sixteenth-century biblical commonwealths of New England. In the Massachusetts Bay Colony, just as in the Europe of Saint Thomas Aquinas, the religious and the secular were so fused that the churches dominated education and the area we would call "welfare work," and they also considerably influenced art, science, technology, and politics. Secular agencies for handling these matters had not yet matured, and the Church filled the gap by taking on strictly earthly functions. For its part, Vatican II rejected the sort of radical secularization that declares Christianity irrelevant and the secular order absolutely independent of the Gospel. But it also clearly ratified the relative autonomy of that same secular world with its "own laws and values which must be gradually deciphered, put to use, and regulated by men. . . ."[6]

The years immediately following the Second Vatican Council were not, however, an opportune time for codifying the theory of Catholic education—supposing that this could be done even in the best of times. For as the 1960s began, enormous waves of change were gathering and were about to break over the shores of comfortably familiar and accepted Catholic concepts. But despite the fears of many anxious hearts, these forces would not really strike at the essentials of Christian faith itself. For the great winds and tides of autumn do not fundamentally diminish the land and sea and sky. Indeed, they disclose new aspects of these realities and compel us to look at them afresh. At the same time, they do radically alter the coastline so that a map of the old landmarks and harbors is no longer much help. And here we may find some analogy to the impact on the Catholic community of the religious events of our age.

The most serious effect of these events has been an actual crisis of faith for a good many people. Almost anyone who reads the papers is aware of this. The Protestant theologian John Macquarrie remarked, in a review of a collection of statements called *Married Priests and Married Nuns:* "One sometimes wonders whether the Roman Catholic Church is in process of renewal or whether we are witnessing its dissolution."[7] But a Catholic who may be quite conscious of the turbulence that prompts observations of this sort should also be confident that the Church will survive, although he is not expected to predict what external forms or accidental features it may come to have.

The reflective Catholic should be able to distinguish his religious community with its distinctive faith and cult from the outrageous failures of many of its members. He will avoid, therefore, the heated rhetoric of those journalistic symposia which snap: Has the Church a Future? Can One Continue to Accept the Church? For after all, the members of the Church should have, as Pius XII once said, the clear sense not only of belonging to the Church, but of being the Church. This is to say that the Church, like any society, is constituted by its individual members and is not a mysterious entity quite apart from them. But that does not mean that these human persons are free to make of that Church, which confesses Christ to be its Head, whatever they will. Religious freedom, as the German bishops pointed out in a statement on December 27, 1968, is valid "for the personal decision in relation to faith, but it has nothing to do with determining the content and scope of divine revelation." In similar fashion, the people of the United States are not free to junk the Constitution either in theory or in practice if they propose to remain loyal to the ends and means of life in the American republic as its founders understood these.

There is an important distinction to be made, therefore, between the substance of this Church which preaches the Gospel and the brutal particulars thrown up against the sky by the misunderstandings and sins even of its loyal adherents. Paul was unhappy with the spots and wrinkles in the first-century Church, and in no century will the Church mirror the Gospel flawlessly. This should hardly surprise us, since neither Washington nor Bronxville nor the South Bronx come near embodying our far less demanding national ideals. The distinction here is not only real, but it has been clearly acknowledged by some very radical Catholics as well as by more conventional ones. There was, for instance, Camilo Torres, the revolutionary priest killed by the Colombian army while he was serving with guerrillas in 1966. On one occasion when he was praised for his fierce criticism of the social backwardness of the Church in Colombia, he objected: "I am a Christian. I believe, I am a priest. I love the Church. My criticisms are directed against accidental aspects."[8] Or, as the writer of a letter to the editor of the English Catholic weekly, *The Tablet,* succinctly stated: *"Sir:* The behaviour of St. Peter's boat often makes me feel sick, but I do not step off into the sea."[9]

Nevertheless, the failures of individual Christians do badly compromise Christianity, just as the failures of individual Americans compromise our national ideals. The angry recognition of such failures may contribute to an atmosphere of crisis, but it may also provide some hope for the future. There are, after all, two ways of looking at the present suffering and stress. We can imagine a person saying to himself a decade ago, "Well, there are problems here and there in the life of the Church which need attention." But after a year or two more had passed, this reckoning would have begun to appear absurdly inadequate. By the mid-1960s it no longer seemed to be a question of localized crises to be put out like so many brush fires. This was conflagration—what Paul VI once called an hour of total decision. For now we are seen to be living in one of those historic moments when a profound tremor shakes the consciousness of the whole human family, and the Church in the world is scarcely immune. If anything, it registers this shock all the more keenly because it is aware both of time and eternity, knowing what human nature historically is and what it aspires to become.

Yet that imagery of crisis and flames is not only lurid but misleadingly negative. We see this when we recall that the Church, although it is a special sort of society, is uniquely free of confinement to any one era or place. It is a true community because it is the effecting of an association, even across national boundaries, of persons united, however imperfectly at times, by a common faith and purpose. This produces, in turn, certain shared experiences as well as the creation over the centuries of liturgical and institutional forms that express and serve that faith and purpose. Some of these forms are evangelical in origin and some are not. The New Testament speaks of the priesthood and the Eucharist but not of cardinals and concordats. The Church can, therefore, accomplish dramatic changes in its appearance, and it has done so.

In recent centuries, for instance, devout Catholics may have supposed that the Church's governance was necessarily so centralized that the pope dealt with many matters affecting local churches. But this was not at all the pattern in the first eleven centuries. The movement toward centralization, which got so big a push from Hildebrand (Pope Saint Gregory VII), has had definite advantages. For one thing, it has provided a check on parochialism or tyranny at the diocesan level. But it is not incapable of modification. Nowadays, indeed, there is a renewed emphasis on the idea of the whole episcopal "college"—the Roman pontiff, together with all the other bishops—as the full successor to the authority and responsibilities of the Lord's Apostles. This accent on collegiality may significantly alter the practices of centralization. It has already stimulated the pope's consulting of bishops, the bishops' consulting of the priests and other people of their dioceses, and the pastors' consulting of their parishioners. Not that this has solved all problems. We hear, in fact, of parish councils refusing to approve new carpeting for the rectory or refusing to invite to the parish school the disadvantaged children of another neighborhood. The first decision was trivial but the second was not, and the teaching sisters of the school in question resigned.

These incidents are tiny indices reminding us that over two millennia the Church has shown that she is not by her essence nearly so bound to specific cultural and legal forms as, let us say, the Athenian democracy or the United States Senate have necessarily been. From the world in which Catholics found themselves, they often borrowed legal or ritual structures for their own organization and worship. Sometimes they did this too enthusiastically and sometimes too slowly; in both cases, a correction was later on required. Paul VI, speaking on January 28, 1971, to officials of the Roman tribunals, remarked: "It is unfortunately true that the Church . . . has in the course of the centuries borrowed from civil legislations certain serious imperfections, even methods which were unjust in the true and proper sense, at least objectively speaking."[10] Such borrowings were now being sloughed off; but one day earlier, on the other side of the world, another kind of adaptation, once forbidden, was serenely under way. On Taiwan, the exiled archbishop of Nanking marked the Chinese New Year with the traditional rites honoring Heaven and the ancients. The seventeenth-century missionaries had allowed these rites, but Rome,

under the impression that they were idolatrous, had then pro-
scribed them. Some writers, in their anxiety to make the point we
are underlining here, have exaggerated it by insisting that the
Church is not a society but a movement. But although it is surely
not a society identified with any one civilization, race, or locale,
neither is it a movement in the sense in which Platonism or even
Marxism is. It is, if you like, a society that moves: a people on the
march—what Saint Paul called "the Israel of God." Should this be
forgotten, the balance may have to be righted by stressing whatever element has currently been underplayed.

For this reason, a more attractive image for the contemporary
situation is one suggested by an analogy Cardinal Newman once
made. The Church should ideally resemble a great river flowing
through history. But a hundred or more years ago, many well-
intentioned Catholics, including popes, bishops, and determined
layfolk, decided that it would be better if the Church were to
resemble a lake; and to achieve this effect they created an immense dam out of firmly held convictions and practices. But the
Church remained what it truly is, and the waters piled up until the
dam was inevitably swept away. Since it broke only yesterday, we
are still astonished by the sight of a torrent in which roofs and
logs and chicken coops bob madly up and down. Yet if we only
think of it, we shall judge it fortunate that the Church has resumed
its appropriate character of a river moving in and with the story
of the human race. Now the Church more easily understands that
although it is a true society, a community of persons united in a
common faith and shared action, still it is not the kind of society
whose survival requires preserving intact all its historically developed structures, however admirable and ancient these may be.
On the contrary, it has often enough changed these forms, albeit
very gradually at times, and it is doing that very thing today. It is
precisely this fluidity which makes the river metaphor appropriate.

No metaphor is to be strained, of course, but this one does
remind us of the possibility that present events will lead to a
deepening and purifying of the faith and practice of Catholics.
They have already inspired, indeed forced, these Christians to ask
important and sometimes painful questions about themselves and
their belief. This is prompting theologians to develop new con-
ceptual constructs that will express less imperfectly the divine
realities known through this faith. The council, in fact, invited
theologians to do this, noting that "the deposit of faith or revealed
truths is one thing; the manner in which they are formulated without violence to their meaning and significance is another."[11] And
Paul VI, at the close of the council's third session, underscored

one way in which theological understanding develops when he said: "What the Church has taught for centuries is what we teach. The only difference is that something that up to now could be found only in the vital activity of the Church is now clearly expressed as doctrine."[12]

For these very reasons, though, there cannot be many Catholic educators who think it possible at this particular moment to produce a satisfactory account of the meaning of Catholicism for education; indeed, few would suggest that it would be prudent to try. Perhaps in the 1950s many would have believed that the thing could be done, although not, perhaps, by themselves. Today even the clumsiest author would have the sour consolation of knowing that an adequate formulation of the Christian view of education is beyond anyone's reach. The times are not propitious; and if the attempt is made, about all that remains in suspense is the exact degree by which it will fall short, for even a big book will not encompass this great theme.

But given this disspirited preamble, a sharp reader may suggest that the appropriate course is indicated by Lao-tzu's bleak epigram: "Those who know do not speak; those who speak do not know." Whoever is unwilling to take this hint should nevertheless be mannerly enough not to begin on a low note of whine. If he insists on writing about Catholicism and education, he should maintain a decent reserve about the hardships of the job and his own limitations. This would be very sensibly said, and this chapter may well conclude by indicating why this essay is done and some of the tactics to be used.

Meditation on the aims of Christian education is worthwhile— at least for the meditators. It is often said that each generation needs to mentally reorganize and rewrite history for itself, and this holds for certain other matters. If a generation hopes to arrive at any wisdom, it must make some philosophical and theological reflection on its experience, even if only to conclude glumly that life is absurd and religion an opiate. Thus a Christian in any age, and surely not least in ours, should brood over certain basic and formidable questions. He ought to ask himself what his religious convictions mean for that complicated and life-long process we call education. Not to do so would condemn him to lasting ignorance of whether he was dealing in his action with ends or means or with sheer irrelevancies. He would flounder without realizing it, and his case would be like that ascribed by a Vietnamese to the Americans in his country who had, he said, only measures and not a policy.[13]

Even if we achieve little by way of a policy, the effort to arrive at one should teach us something. That effort will go through several stages, meeting with a number of distinctive obstacles. In the next chapter, therefore, we stop to consider certain of these hindrances, because that is one way of casting light on our topic itself. We speak about the nature and difficulties of educational theorizing in general and of theorizing about Christian education in particular. Our pages are liberally sprinkled with allusions to persons and sources, but this is not an exercise in name-dropping. One of two purposes is to be served. At times, mindful of the classic warning that categories without experience are empty, we hope to draw abstractions about education a bit closer to earth through concrete illustration.

A second group of citations is much more essential because, if I write about the relevance of Catholicism for education, my task is quite different from that of a philosopher. My prime obligation is to say what the Catholic society, this people gathered into a church, thinks or should think about education in light of its belief. I am not now advancing my own readings of human experience; rather, I am speaking for a religious faith that is neither my invention nor my exclusive possession. I must try to give a loyal account of the Catholic tradition in education and its efforts to adapt itself to new understandings and the needs of new times. It is like being asked to say what Americans should think about education in light of their national ideals and history. Of course, my transcription is not an official one. But it would be worthless if it did not strive to be honestly representative. As often as the limits of a small book allow, then, I quote from the weightiest voices of contemporary Catholicism—chiefly from the documents of the Second Vatican Council and the statements of recent popes —to indicate that the readings here are not intended to be idiosyncratic but to reflect the mind of the Catholic community.

NOTES

1. "Pastoral Constitution on the Church in the Modern World," promulgated on December 7, 1965, and quoted here from the English translation in *The Documents of Vatican II*, Walter M. Abbott, S.J., gen. ed. (New York: Guild-American-Association Presses, 1966), n. 77, p. 289.
2. *Ibid.*, n. 44, p. 246.
3. Quoted by H. J. Maidenberg, "Black Power Movement Spreading in Caribbean," the *New York Times*, November 9, 1969, p. 1.
4. The quotation from the *American Weekly Mercury* comes from Robert Francis Seybolt, *Source Studies in American Colonial Education: The Private School* (Urbana: University of Illinois Press, 1925), p. 103. For

the questions of the school children, see Ruth V. Byler *et al.,* eds., *Teach Us What We Want to Know: Report of a survey on health interests, concerns, and problems of 5,000 students in selected schools from kindergarten through grade twelve* (New York: Published for the Connecticut State Board of Education by the Mental Health Materials Center, 1969), pp. 26, 27, 43, 90, *et passim.*

5. See the essay by T. S. Eliot, "Religion Without Humanism," in Norman Foerster, ed., *Humanism and America: Essays on the Outlook of Modern Civilisation* (New York: Farrar and Rinehart, 1930), pp. 106–108.

6. "Pastoral Constitution on the Church in the Modern World," *The Documents of Vatican II, op. cit.,* n. 36, p. 233.

7. See the review by John Macquarrie of *Married Priests and Married Nuns,* in the *New York Times Book Review,* September 29, 1968, p. 63.

8. Quoted in German Guzman, *Camilo Torres,* trans. John D. Ring (New York: Sheed and Ward, 1969), p. 120.

9. Letter signed Philip Hagreen, Lingfield, Surrey, published in *The Tablet,* 225 (September 25, 1971), 939.

10. Quoted from the text of Paul VI's address as given in *L'Osservatore Romano,* weekly English edition, February 11, 1971, p. 7.

11. "Pastoral Constitution on the Church in the Modern World," *The Documents of Vatican II, op. cit.,* n. 62, pp. 268–269.

12. Paul VI, quoted in *The Documents of Vatican II, op. cit.,* p. 396, n. 1.

13. Quoted by Robert Shaplen, "Letter from Saigon," *The New Yorker,* 44 (June 29, 1968), 38.

2

Taking Some Bearings:
Reflections on Educational Theory

You have come to talk to me about the philosophy of education. There is no such thing. Good morning.

Robert Lowe, nineteenth-century
English politician to a
school inspector

Educational theory is a case. Many people like to try their hand at it, and logically it should be of considerable importance, since education is so central to human existence. Nevertheless, an English reviewer once remarked that the subject called "philosophy of education" has lacked a satisfactory image; but, he added generously, this does not mean that it has to be an unprofitable bore.[1] If it often seems to be, this is partly because it must contend with some formidable impediments—some of them intrinsic to the activity itself and some of them due to its contemporary social setting. These are worth looking at in some detail, for the present book is an exercise in educational theory, although it does not belong to the same category as most of the studies described as philosophies of education. Those works generally aim to develop the implications for education of one or other formal philosophy: Idealism, Existentialism, Pragmatism, or Realism. Catholic Christianity, on the other hand, is a religion and not at all a philosophy in this technical sense.[2] Of course, there have been Catholic philosophers whose thought was powerfully influenced by their religious experience, although their philosophy itself was not a deduction from their faith but essentially the work of their reflection on life. Therefore, a book might be written on the significance for education of Theistic Realism as sifted through the intelligence of Augustine, or Thomas Aquinas, or Newman, or Blondel, or Teilhard de Chardin. But all these thinkers would have been properly appalled if we tried to identify their philosophies with Catholicism itself or their reasonings with the faith that informed their lives as Christians.

On the other hand, although Catholicism is not a philosophy, it certainly does include an interpretation of man and his nature and purposes, his history, and the conditions of his actual existence. So we should expect Catholicism to make some difference for education. In fact, we can distill from it some elements of an educational theory or at least some norms for guiding practice and appraising it. Of course, there will be plenty of hard school questions for which Catholicism as such provides no distinctive answers nor any special tools for analyzing the concepts involved, although individual Catholics may provide both. This is why documents like Pius XI's encyclical of 1929 on "Christian Education of Youth" or even the more nuanced "Declaration on Christian Education" of Vatican II thirty-six years later can seem disappointing to those who look to them for a full-fledged philosophy of education. Yet they do contain fragments of educational theory because they say something about what education should be in the light of what faith, and reason enlightened by faith, propose that human life should be.

It is just this kind of effort to say what education ought to be that people find both perennially attractive and often curiously unsatisfactory. A sliver of historical gossip comes to mind here. On the morning of July 30, 1763, Dr. Johnson and Boswell went sculling on the Thames. During their conversation Johnson said that a knowledge of Greek and Latin is essential for any sound education. This prompted him to ask the boy who was rowing what he would give to know about the Argonauts and the boy replied: "Sir, I would give what I have." "Much pleased" with so brave an answer, Johnson added a gloss of his own for Boswell: 'Every human being, whose mind is not debauched, will be willing to give all that he has to get knowledge.' "

Now although Johnson was a genius, he was hardly exceptional in this fondness for theorizing about education. In any event, he would not seem so nowadays when a good many people spend a good deal of time expounding their notions of what schools should be doing. The incident reported by Boswell is recalled, therefore, not because it is special but because it is typical. It also nicely suggests the way in which talk about educational practice glides easily into spacious and confident statements not only about educational theory but about life and destiny. Naturally enough. For practical school problems always invoke, if only faintly and negatively, the application to the academic business at hand of a controlling idea or view of the world. Sometimes, to tell the truth, it is rather a defeatist idea. Fred Allen, telling an audience at Brandeis about his years in Boston's High School of Commerce, remarked: "A Commerce education really never interfered with anything you had planned to do in later life. You just majored in adolescence for your four years." But the joke contained a kernel of social criticism in its tacit claim to have identified the concept of education-as-custody embodied in that school.

An influential concept need not be, indeed rarely is, fully unfurled into a systematic philosophy. It may amount to no more than a broad perspective or basic attitude. One man, for example, may hold that religious instruction and worship should be effectively linked with elementary schooling, whereas his neighbor believes that they positively should not. In either case, there is a strong conviction that makes a difference for education. It is because nearly everyone has some such convictions about life and education that nearly everyone has a fragmentary educational theory.

But something fuller, more precise, and more systematic, is intended by people who teach and write in the field of philosophy of education.[3] They might, of course, confine themselves to a survey of the great theorists from Plato to Dewey, or even to a chapter-by-chapter exegesis of *Democracy and Education.* But if they are more ambitious, they may well aim at developing the implications for education of the method and findings of a formal philosophy. Of course, philosophy in the Western world alone has been marvelously heterogeneous, running, as it does, from the pre-Socratics to the linguistic analysts. Yet the hundreds of philosophies that have been devised share an interest in certain perennial questions about man and the universe—even if they only hope to dissolve these questions by taking their terms apart. Thus they have relevance for education and particularly for clarification of the objectives of formal schooling and the values it presumably serves. This concern for aims and values distinguishes philosophy of education from the study of those earthy school issues that require a largely practical solution. For instance, although we might be guided by antecedent hunches, we can hardly determine which of several ways of teaching mathematics would be best for a particular class at a particular time except by trying them out. On the other hand, we find ourselves moving in the headier atmosphere of educational theory, if we accept Plato's invitation in the *Republic* to consider whether mathematics is not especially valuable for converting the soul from a blinding preoccupation with the world of matter and change to the contemplation of truth and being. No doubt, we could hardly decide that question, either, without recourse to a test by experience; but the question itself is of an order different from the strictly pedagogical one of methods. We might also ask Instrumentalism what it has to say about the relative weight to be given the literary and scientific humanities in high school, or we might ask Theistic Realism how its ethical theory would judge racial segregation in schools, or we might ask each of them what is meant by "learning."

But to affirm the existence of educational theory is not to say that its existence is comfortable. Quite the contrary. Sometimes the very notion of philosophizing about education is attacked as a disagreeable delusion. *Time* once remarked approvingly that in the military services's teacher-training programs there was no such nonsense as "philosophy of education" courses, the term itself being distrustingly enclosed between quotation marks. Sidney Hook has agreeably observed that to encourage philosophers to derive an educational theory from some established philosophical position like Idealism, Thomism, or Pragmatism is to encourage them to perpetrate garrulous absurdities.[4] *Éppur si muove.* People do theorize about education, and there is more than one philosophy of education, just as there is more than one view of the world.

Often enough, though, observers are more irritated by the manner in which philosophy of education is done than by its matter. For instance, any such philosophy will have a lot to say about moral values because all serious educational practice is, at bottom, the attempt to actualize an ideal of the good man. All the greatest theoreticians have been moralists who knew that men seek happiness; and all were sure that we cannot be authentically happy without being good. Consequently, these philosophers spent a great deal of time trying to define human felicity and goodness and to show how education is to promote them. This obliged them to think of goals lying ahead and of the means for reaching them. To tell the truth, even the most traditional and least speculative forms of schooling are not without a strong futuristic and instrumental strain. Locke, for example, would have the sons of seventeenth-century gentlemen taught fencing and law because these were required for good breeding and their adult occupations. But music, he said, could be given last place.

In short, to take education seriously is to take seriously questions about ends and means, values and the Good. Yet to be effective, such considerations must be made with grace and insight. Otherwise the academicians will start growling and the plain citizens will ignore the whole business. In a cross footnote in *The*

American University, Jacques Barzun complained that there are hundreds of deplorable books on education. He was especially disenchanted by a certain "Philosophy of Education" for having said, among other things judged foolish, that the "problem of aims in education is a problem of *values.*"[5] But it is, of course; and the wretched writer who annoyed Mr. Barzun can properly be faulted only for a lack of sophistication in repeating a familiar but still useful truth.

The most persistent criticism, however, is the hardest to refute because it fastens on what may very well be a connatural limitation of all educational theory. For when this theory is truly speculative, it is apt to seem irrelevant; and when it gets down to practical issues, it does not seem philosophical. All writers of treatises on education are hard put to elude the horns of this melancholy dilemma. Shall they suffocate their readers by a tiresome encyclopedism that strains to deduce solutions for specific school problems 'from philosophical analyses of man and learning? Or shall they bore those readers by marooning them on a level of high generalization where there may be, indeed, a few important points to be made but small hope of making them effectively in a climate so rarefied?

In some matters, the purely theoretical consideration is compelling enough. The historian finds the moral issue posed by the atomic bombing of Hiroshima still relevant, even though the moment of decision is long past. A public official may ponder the ethical question confronting him in the offer of a subtly masked bribe, which he nevertheless intends to accept. But in education, theory separated from practice seems shadowy because education is preeminently a real activity in the real world. Although they have philosophical presuppositions, the great problems always seem to be practical ones, demanding a practically workable solution. Accordingly, on January 13, 1971, the *New York Times* published a gloomy editorial on the low estate of reading performance in the city's schools, noting that: "The first priority for research is to concentrate not on educational theories but on observation of successful action in the field, with a view to making the success contagious."

An original mind occasionally escapes the dilemma here by a powerful, although inevitably one-sided, realization of a few fundamental insights that enable it effectively to connect the general with the specific. In *The School and Society,* for instance, John Dewey produced a small classic through a single-minded concentration on one dominant aim (growth in selfhood through participation in a democratically organized society), achieved principally through one pedagogical technique (problem-solving, especially in shared arts and crafts, as a prime method of developing children's intelligence and character). Since he did not otherwise descend much to particulars, the book has a timeless air and remains accessible. But most writers cannot hope to construct so much out of variations on so few themes. Besides, even Dewey did not perfectly solve the problem of being both philosophical and comprehensively relevant.

There is a magnetism about the directness with which Dewey's total philosophy established organic bonds between concrete recommendations for school action and a general metaphysic and epistemology. From his abstract theses about the nature of the universe, life, man, and value, he could make issue precise directives for the content and method of elementary schooling.

But it was, after all, for a handful of favored children, mostly the sons and daughters of university people, that the school described in *The School and Society* was created. A reader could not guess from the pages of any of Dewey's main books on education that these were written at a time when the ideals of democratic public education were being traduced by a biracial school system imposed by law in the South and by injurious custom in the North. In fact, well into the 1950s, American philosophers of education were almost universally silent on the whole matter of biracialism. This may have been because their thought moved within the technical framework of formal philosophies and did not easily encounter the tragic realities of American life. Nonetheless, the issues raised by the segregated public school were moral ones that should naturally have concerned the philosopher of education.

This philosopher needs, therefore, remarkable powers of insight, discrimination, and rhetoric, if he is to keep his head in the sky but his feet firmly on earth. If he details recipes for current problems, he runs that aforesaid risk of becoming swiftly outmoded as the issues are resolved or as they acquire a new shape. Even when the problem is perennial, it is hard to demonstrate any distinctive link between a particular philosophy and a determined procedure. We can just as easily construct a rationale for learning-by-doing from Thomism as from Dewey's Experimentalism.

On the other hand, if the theorist confines himself to what can be reasonably asserted about ends and means in education within the perspectives supplied by his general philosophy, he is apt to strike literate readers as dreary and trite. He may try to evade stereotyping by leaping aboard a wildly original notion and advocating the abolition of all schools, the teaching of calculus to babies, or the forced conversion of the American citizenry to scientific humanism or to the Freudianism of Summerhill. But, if he does, informed persons will be likely to judge him either ignorant or dishonest.

We must conclude that just because education is as wide as life itself and its concept nearly as comprehensive, there are not very many universal predications that can safely be made of it, and the few there are seem dreadfully hard to formulate freshly. It is even harder to show in reasonable detail what effective contribution these general propositions can make toward dispelling the swarm of actual problems that harass education in our time, if not in every time.

THE CULTURAL CONTEXT OF CONTEMPORARY EDUCATIONAL THEORY

If theorizing about education always involves risks, the climate of contemporary civilization makes that venture particularly chancy, just as the religious situation complicates the attempt to formulate a Christian educational theory. This is because the educational process is basically the process of passing on a people's way of life, and the American way of life is, at this moment, gripped by convulsive change with all its attendant tensions and uncertainties. Our civilization has also reached an unprecedented peak of complexity, which means that it is harder than ever to evaluate it properly, discerning what is good and to be enhanced; what is ambiguous and to be purified; what is evil and to be overcome. But the more problematic the way of life, the more bewildering is the task of education and the business of philosophizing about it.

We should note, perhaps, that to speak of education as the transmission of a way of life does not necessarily imply a mandarin immobility and hostility to change. People may esteem independence and innovation, as Americans profess to do, and then they will expect education to instill these attitudes and universities and research institutes to explore the unknown. *Transmit* may be a clumsy term; but it remains true that education, as Dewey put it in *Democracy and Education,* is the means of social continuity. Ordinary experience proves as much. If we look about us, we see a legion of phenomena that are called education in one sense or another: young parents teaching their first baby to walk and to convert its genial growls into words; mothers at park playgrounds making sure their toddlers learn how to coexist with one another; teachers in classrooms or shops or labs and clergymen in pulpits; a sophisticated secretarial school teaching girls not only how to type but how to dress for a Wall Street firm; Spanish Harlem's

Young Lords inducting a recruit; a master plumber showing an apprentice how to thread a pipe; mothers helping sweating little daughters turn out their first batch of cookies and fathers showing sons how to use a saw; a lecturer performing for a thousand freshmen in a California state university, and another sitting with a handful of people around a table in a Harvard graduate seminar.

We might tell one of those handy visitors from Mars, who are an obliging audience for such explanations, that these are all examples of what we call *education.* But what description will be ample enough to cover these and all other possible instances? We may concede that young people do a certain amount of educating of one another and that every man educates himself to some extent; yet in most cases we can still say that education finds an older person helping a younger one acquire some skill, information, or attitude—or, at least, helping him get started on that process of self-education. And then we may agree that Christopher Dawson's formulation is a neat one: "Taken in its widest sense education is simply the process by which the new members of a community are initiated into its ways of life and thought from the simplest elements of behaviour or manners up to the highest tradition of spiritual wisdom."[6]

If a society is to survive at all, its substance must somehow be passed from the older to the younger members of the group. To say as much is neither to define what that substance may be nor how it is to be handed on. There is no sanction here for the antiquated and destructive concept of teaching as the pouring of knowledge into students who are moulded like clay pots and then filled up. Neither is there any sanction for the notion that education must inevitably support the status quo. On the contrary, even the most traditional educations have been to some degree reconstructive. There was always a momentous passage when the tribe began to substitute agriculture for aimless food gathering. In nations pervaded by a dynamic of change, education may be literally traditional and yet far from static. For if a society, by choice or necessity, puts a premium on adventuresome and pragmatic qualities and encourages criticism and a restless zeal for improvement, then these will be among the principal attitudes learned by the rising generation—to the discomfort, sometimes, of its parents and other teachers. American civilization has, of course, subscribed to these ideals in theory from its beginnings. It will be remembered that President Eisenhower used to like to call his economics "dynamic conservatism"!

But nowadays our society's metabolic rate has greatly accelerated. Although we are not sure whether this marks a building up or a breaking down of its system, we do know that we live in a period of change so enormous that it appears to be nearly total—which, of course, it is not. The larger part of life remains constant and people are born, grow up, marry, beget, work, suffer, and die, today as yesterday. Nevertheless, the element of change is relatively so dominant that it nearly fills our consciousness and leaves us as preoccupied by it as children at the zoo by their first sight of an elephant. Thus we are constantly remarking this phenomenon of change to one another and endlessly enumerating and diagnosing its conditions. Although the actual crises perdure with doomsday intensity, there are by now simply no new words to be used to sum them up in a compelling way.

No doubt we should remind ourselves that American life has always had a measure of hardness. Existence on the frontier was mean enough, with lynchings and eye-gouging tavern brawls and housewives on the Plains scooping up buffalo dung for fuel. It is not sure that our current distress has yet reached the desperate pitch of the 1860s or the 1930s; moreover, the signs of our times, as of every time, include at least some that are modestly hopeful as Charles A. Reich and Jean-François Revel have discovered.[7] Yet we suspect that Americans of earlier generations had a greater certainty about the ultimate meanings of public and private life and the relationship of the one to the other. They had, consequently, a greater if more naïve certainty about educational objectives than we do. Since they saw life within a firm framework of significance, they were able to define the school's task securely.

St. Jean de Crèvecoeur voiced the sanguine spirit of the young republic when he looked forward to the nineteenth century and found the prospect good. "Americans are the western pilgrims," he wrote a year before the Treaty of Paris; and according to his report, their caravan was by no means mournful. On the contrary, it was loaded with exuberance. Americans were the westward voyagers to a rich, nearly untouched continent that lay before them like a Promised Land. Seizing this prize would be hard work but also exhilarating because it was a pioneer venture whose success seemed assured. Thus Crèvecoeur could describe the Americans as men who had been liberated from despotism, poverty, and servitude and were now industrious, prosperous, and self-assured in the jolly company of their "fat and frolicsome" wives and children. They seemed to him to have found themselves a whole new set of principles, ideas, and opinions. In fact, these were not substantially original but largely the fresh bottling of a classical or European vintage, embellished with new emphases and nuances and a new confidence. It seemed as though the ideals born in ancient Israel or Greece would now have their depths sounded more effectively than ever before. For decades, therefore, and despite bitter trials, Americans appear to have had considerable surety about their goals and the possibility of achieving them. They had not learned to doubt the vision itself, nor had they been overcome by tedium at the thought of striving for it. While they could believe in that vision, they could transfigure the harshness of daily existence.

We see this in the life and work of that astonishing personality known as Grandma Moses, who presented the phenomenon of an artistic sensibility formed in the nineteenth century but flowering only much later and marvelously surviving down to the 1960s. Anna Mary Robertson Moses was still engaged in her poetic painting when she triumphantly celebrated her one hundredth birthday in 1960. Professional crosspatches fault her art, but everyone else loves it. We would surely misunderstand her if we supposed that she painted literal pictures of things as they were. Grandma Moses used symbols of a vanished, rural world to evoke, along with the memory of the past, the dream of a peaceable kingdom not yet seen on earth. Still, the very titles she gave her pictures suggest a time when life was not only simpler but somehow purer and better than it is now: Childhood Home, Early Springtime on the Farm, Father's Mill in Summer, Going to Church, Shenandoah Valley, Applebutter Making at the Dudley Place. The pictures themselves, although created by a very old person, are of a world paradisically young—the skies so blue, the grass so green, the animated people casting no shadows. The artist's own life had not been easy. She hired out when she was only a girl and worked hard all during a life so long that she outlived most of her ten children. But recalling the century of her own childhood, she could say as she memorialized it: "What fun we had!"

This is hardly the message of painters whose sensibilities were shaped, wholly or in part, since World War I. They have turned from figurative painting to reflect the consciousness of this era by giving us their impression of its inner reality—a highly troubled view of a highly troubling world. The surrealist paints nightmares and the pop artist formalizes the designs of soup cans and bathroom fixtures. The abstractionists and action painters eschew the human form for swirling lines and throbbing slabs of color like cauldrons of anxieties or geometric figures whose glacial remoteness suggests an arctic of the spirit. Even those artists who create a recognizable world discover it to be tinged with a profound sadness. Loneliness and melancholy brood over Edward Hopper's empty streets and Andrew Wyeth's austere landscapes. But no cause for surprise here. We expect artists to refract through their temperaments the prevailing conviction and mood of their day, and in recent decades civilization has seemed to many thoughtful people to be increasingly beleaguered. Whether this judgment is correct does not matter, so far as shaping the intellectual climate goes, if it is the one commonly formed.

"We happen to live," said President John F. Kennedy at a news conference on October 11, 1961, "in the most dangerous time in the history of the human race." Since the prospect has not notably brightened since then, we can easily understand why imaginative work today is preoccupied with suffering, disorder, and meaninglessness. Life currently confronts the artist with some very desperate data indeed. We are all steadily bombarded with the threat that if nuclear war does not blast human society to pieces, its own internal stresses may do the job nearly as well. Even if these problems are not essentially unique, their magnitude and intensity are. We know that the homeless are dying tonight in the streets of Calcutta, and if there is a riot in Rome, we hear of it within an hour. When Boston was shelled during the Revolution, it was certainly fearful for its inhabitants, and Abigail Adams wrote to her husband that the incessant cannonading made it impossible to sleep and eat. But the farmers in the Berkshires were remote from it all and, in any case, the noisy interruption of mealtime would have been counted a trivial affliction by those whose lives were ripped apart in twentieth-century wars.

We hear often enough that Western civilization is in a bad way. But then we also sometimes hear that it is doing fairly well. It remains disputed whether our problems arise because civilization is overly mechanized or not mechanized enough; because scientists do not care about the ideas of literary humanists, because nonscientific humanists know nothing about science, or because most people know nothing about either. It is announced that democracy and an authentic religiousness are gaining while despotism and doctrinaire materialism decline, or it is announced that it is just the other way round. Some philosophers insist that our troubles stem from the failure of our moral development to keep pace with our technological progress; others retort that we are in difficulty because we have not yet devised the technological means of realizing our matured and purified ethical insight. In any case, even the most casual reader of the newspapers is bound to think that the world is getting ever more deeply lost in a wood and nobody has a compass. Indeed, the sheer size and intricacy of domestic and foreign problems seem to make solution impossible, and even a constructive comment unlikely.

This sketchy reference to the current scene is made for the sake of underlining the difficulties besetting contemporary efforts to construct a philosophy of education. For all these problems have inevitable repercussions on schools, particularly at the higher levels, where there is the greatest sensitivity to the quakings in the wider civic society. Thus we hear about the problems of the big-city systems and the problems of suburban schools; about the problems of nonpublic education, the problems of high schools, and the truly appalling pressures on colleges and universities. Curricula are under attack and teaching styles criticized. Students are in revolt or desperate. The faculty is demoralized; the administration is sparring frantically, and parents are both baffled and alarmed. There is much talk about all this, but a good deal of it is guff. We are reminded of that twelfth-century teacher whose classes Peter Abelard attended. This man, said Abelard smartly, had plenty of words but no sense, and "when he lit the fire, he filled the house with smoke, not with light."[8]

Public problems have by now so engulfed the individual consciousness that a single intelligence could construct a complete theory of education only if it were that of a genius furnished with universal erudition or if it abstracted entirely from the realities of today. It is likely to be some time, therefore, before the philosophy of education acquires that satisfactory image it has been said to lack. For if schooling is always hard work and theorizing about education always a tricky business, these activities are more than ordinarily risky when the civilization the schools mirror and serve is in a spasm like that which attends the death of one era and the birth of another. The enterprise of education can scarcely be fully expounded when we still know so little about the meaning and direction of our overwhelming contemporary experiences.

CATHOLIC EDUCATIONAL THEORY AND ITS PROBLEMS

If it is hard nowadays to get the theme of education itself into clear focus, it is still harder to outline even impressionistically the reality to which the term *Catholicism* points. Yet we must try if we want to talk about Catholicism's significance for education. The next chapter represents just such an attempt, but first we want to mention the ambushes encircling the effort to spell out the relationship of the Gospel to education.

To begin, we might recall something already noted. We said that a Christian teacher should ideally have a reasonably full theory of education that would combine harmoniously the contributions of philosophy and religious faith. In this case he would have arrived at a synoptic view in which a generalized theory of the aims, curricula, methods, and agencies of education is logically and fruitfully related to a complete view of life and value. But he will not have built this synthesis entirely or even chiefly from his faith and its theological elucidation in the Christian community over the past two millennia.

There are many theoretical and practical questions about education to which the Gospel does not speak directly. It does not, for instance, umpire the dispute between those who would teach reading phonetically and those who would emphasize word-recognition. Neither does it affirm the wisdom or the folly of establishing a Christian university in a particular place at a particular time, although it does indeed affirm a concept of human life and destiny which may help people decide whether to establish such a university. In making their decision they would do well to speculate a bit about education, and for that they will need the resources of philosophy and sociology as well as theology. This is to say that just as Christians may be philosophers, so they may also be theorists of education. If they are, they will necessarily draw heavily on moral philosophy, epistemology, and philosophical anthropology. They will often deal with problems common to all educators and sift evidence available to any investigator. Quite likely they will disagree among themselves as heatedly as Thomists, Scotists, and Suarezians have disagreed even while sharing that philosophical consensus known as Scholasticism.

Yet many of the perennial educational problems have religious connotations; therefore, certain theoretical approaches to or practical solutions for these problems should be characteristic of Christians, even though these are not actually distilled from their faith. The Gospel, for instance, says nothing about the founding of schools; but we are scarcely surprised to find that Christians have been interested in formal education, that is, in schooling, ever since the first centuries. No doubt, they began with a concern for their own children and their upbringing at home. In fact, one of the earliest texts dealing with education is from Ignatius of Antioch, who spoke to this point at the opening of the second century: "Fathers, 'bring up your children in the nurture and admonition of the Lord,' and teach them the Holy Scriptures, and also trades, that they may not indulge in idleness."[9]

But, from the first, Christians were also conscious of the obligation laid on them by the Lord to share their faith horizontally across the face of the earth and vertically down the succeeding ages; and whenever people feel strongly about their values, they are apt to start setting up schools. History furnishes all kinds of illustrations of this impulse working on a small and individual scale or on a large and social scale. Michael and Sarah Stein, American friends of Matisse, were so taken with that painter's work that they subsidized an academy in which apprentices might learn from him. Ever since Plato and Aristotle, philosophers have turned to teaching as the best way of introducing their ideas to their contemporaries. Leaders of young nations are usually zealous for the building of elementary schools, as we see in the cases of Jefferson in 1787, or Marcos in the Philippines and Nyerere in Tanzania nearly two centuries later. It is not remarkable, then, to find that Christians have had and still have a similar enthusiasm for formal education. Indeed, it would be misleading to say without explanation that Christianity does not require the conducting of schools. This is true in terms of the essence itself and at the level of abstract theory. But the actual historical experience of the Church has shown that some kind of school program is a practical necessity. This need not, to be sure, take the form of a parochial school system like that which American Catholics have known. But that system has certainly been one specific response to the timeless need for providing a means of achieving the aims of Christian education.

However, if we want to develop a complete theory for this Christian education, certain philosophical stances are bound to appear as incompatible with this purpose. These are the positions that simply cannot become part of the fabric of a Christian "philosophy of education," although their insights can be assimilated once they have been rinsed of the exaggerations they acquired in their original systematic context. A single example may be useful here. On many matters, the Scholastic philosophers disputed acrimoniously among themselves. Yet they all agreed with Plato in thinking that human experience provides data suggesting that our makeup contains an element that is immaterial and therefore deathless. Man indeed is mortal, they would have said, but his spirit is not. It is true that only their religious faith gave them the assurance beyond philosophy that man in his entirety would live again in a restored and unimaginably different life. But from their own philosophical analyses they concluded that the capacity for thought and free choice points to a partial transcendence of the body's inevitable decline and decay. There are contemporary Catholic philosophers, however, who think this goes much too far and that nothing can be known of immortality apart from Christian revelation. Yet even if the medieval Scholastics had not considered demonstrable their thesis about the spirituality of the soul, they would have rejected a strict materialism because it necessarily contradicts the Christian faith in life after death.

In such cases, religious belief functions as a negative norm for testing the soundness of a philosophical hypothesis. But apart from such instances, Catholic philosophers of education, like Catholic political philosophers, will be found building their theories from their diagnoses of experience just like any other thinkers. No doubt, they are persuaded that Christian faith has made them particularly sensitive to certain aspects of this experience. Still, the experience itself is not specialized like that of a physicist in his laboratory; rather, it is of the variety shared by most men. Thus it can easily happen that the educational theories of Catholics will be inferior in one way or another to those of certain other inquirers. This is likely to happen if these Catholics live in times not propitious for particular lines of investigation. The fact that an individual is a convinced Christian does not mean that he automatically develops every virtuality of moral wisdom. Indeed, the era in which he lives may be one in which most people do not even suspect that certain of these virtualities exist. As Teilhard once said, speaking of his vision of the growth of personalism in the universe: "We shall not see it more distinctly than the age of the World allows."[10]

There are plenty of examples to illustrate the point. Saint Thomas Aquinas was not only a theologian of genius but also a dedicated and effective teacher. His little essay "On the Teacher" (*De Magistro*) is a concentrated analysis of one aspect of learning through instruction from another. But today any standard textbook goes far beyond this in its examination of the complete psychology of learning. The Jesuit *Ratio Studiorum* of 1599, although a practical plan for school organization rather than a piece of educational philosophy, was nonetheless designed to guide a Christian school. Inevitably, however, it was a product of its times; and its times were not ripe for full appreciation of democratic social forms or of the importance ascribed by Christianity itself to human freedom and its development in a community.

In contrast, three centuries later, John Dewey spent much of an enormously long career examining the idea of a democratically inspired society. He was clearer, it is true, about the processes to be followed in this society than about the precise content of the idea. Still, the community he described resembled a secularized version of that brotherhood which the Church itself strives to be. In the course of his reflections, Dewey made far more instructive observations about the school's role in nurturing cooperativeness and appreciation of shared responsibility than the Catholic theorists of the late Renaissance ever did. Yet these very virtues are some of the essential social expressions of that love, *charity,* which should be the prime mark of the Christian. But to know a principle is one thing, to grasp all its concrete applications is another. As Vatican II put it: "The Church guards the heritage of God's Word and draws from it religious and moral principles, without always having at hand the solution to particular problems."[11]

It will be agreed, then, that if a Catholic has a full-fledged educational theory, only a segment of it will have been directly derived from his religious convictions. In these pages, again, we are mostly concerned with that precise segment. But this effort to identify Catholicism's implications for ends and means in education is bound to stumble over further obstacles in addition to those encountered by educational theorizing at any time and by American educational theory in these times. It will, for instance, meet in some persons a distrust of the very topic itself. Then as we remarked in the previous chapter, in talking about these ideals we become embarrassed by the ambiguities, not to say scandals, in the lives of those who presumably profess them. Finally, there is that special difficulty of trying to draw a profile of Catholicism at a moment of such extraordinary ferment and theological productivity. We might look at these three hurdles, in the order of their ascending importance, because this is one way of sidling up to the topic of Catholicism and education.

This book aims to speak to all who are interested in educational theory and not just to Catholic Christians; but like any attempt to speak across ideological contexts, it runs up against barriers. In October 1969 the reviewer for Off-Broadway shows for *The New Yorker* was commenting on a new edition of the topical revue, "From the Second City." She concluded her notice by remarking parenthetically: "One question: Why, in enterprises of this sort, are the Jewish jokes so comfortable and homey and we're-all-Jews-here and the Catholic jokes so disparaging."[12]

Perhaps it is because those jokes are aimed at the Church itself or at certain Catholic ideas that arouse more distrust than amusement in the jokesmith. This distrust may be evoked because the ideas themselves are considered harmful or because they are derived from faith and so are regarded with suspicion. For it is certainly true that Catholicism is not a matter of philosophical analyses, hypotheses, and syntheses. It is embodied in the belief and practice of a people who form a distinctive religious community. Of course, this belief has points in common with some philosophies, but essentially it is quite unlike any philosophy.

Philosophers of education offer their conclusions as the fruit of their own thinking, although they naturally owe a debt to those who have influenced them. Their point of departure, as well as the ultimate grounding of their argument, is human experience. This is the experience which implicates us all in manifold relationships within an evolving world of inanimate forces, as well as multiple gradations of life capped by human persons and the complex social structures that are both the necessary milieu of these persons and their own creations. In effect, the philosopher says to his readers: "Do you not agree that this enormous, shifting, mysterious, and multicolored experience of ours is thus-and-so? And if it is, must we not say that only these hypotheses of mine explain it?"

If we have had no such experience as that which this philosopher claims to analyze, or if we find his hypotheses far from reasonable, we shall not ratify his conclusions. The touchstone, in any case, is that common human history of which philosophers offer their personal readings.[13] "Philosophy," wrote Charles S. Peirce in 1898 ". . . is really an experimental science which is common to us all; so that its principal reasonings are not mathematically necessary at all, but are only necessary in the sense that all the world knows beyond all doubt those truths of experience upon which philosophy is founded."[14]

In contrast, that portion of Christian educational theory which is derived from the Gospel is delivered not by philosophy but by religious faith, and this faith is not a profession of abstractions and purely speculative conclusions. It is, for each Christian, a crucial and profoundly personal affirmation about certain historic events and present realities. It affirms, with an assent that should color all life and action, that God exists not within time and space but as their Sole Author and is, therefore, necessarily imperceptible to the senses that are instruments anchored in the world of bodies. By faith, moreover, the Christian not only affirms that God *is* but also that He communicates with men and that this communication, at a determined point in history, took the supreme and unimaginable form of divine incarnation so that Jesus Who lives is authentically God and authentically man.

But Christians must recognize that this persuasion of theirs strikes people who do not share it as bizarre and their allegiance to it as unreasonable, if not outrageous. Indeed, those who are merely nominal Catholics may feel the same way, for they can be caught, like anyone else, by the undertow of disbelief. When Edmund Wilson was at Princeton before World War I, he heard of a young Catholic who commented on the report of a conversation: "I don't see how anybody not brought up to it could swallow it!"[15]

To be sure, it is always hard for people to think or speak about God as real if they are inclined to equate *being* with *material being* and to assume that whatever exists must be visible or have characteristics that can be directly attained by the senses. On the other hand, the philosophical doctrine of analogy—that is to say, partial and proportional similarity—disputes part of this assumption by showing that existence can, in a true sense, be predicated of a reality other than material. With this tool in hand, we might then reflect on the conditions of the world we experience and conclude that there is indeed a Reality beyond this sphere of Whom that predication of existence can be made.

Some of the so-called primitive peoples have gotten well along in this kind of reasoning without formal philosophical instruments. When they lived in a friendly climate, they could quite readily intuit God manifested by the natural splendors of earth and sky. A few decades ago it was reported that certain pygmies of Central Africa had the custom of blowing the first breath of the new day skywards—a symbolic homage, made at dawn to the giver of life. But such insights are less easily available to the urban man, who is no longer close to nature and has not the temperament of a metaphysician. Besides, even if the existence of a supreme and subsistent source of all other being is philosophically asserted, it remains pyschologically almost impossible to conceive of a mind capable of knowing and caring about three billion living human persons. Aristotle could affirm the existence of a Prime Mover, and a tiny trible isolated in the rain forest might comfortably think of God as its Father. But these certainties are hard for men who, on the one hand, know how wide the world is and, on the other, do not find the universe as logical as the Greeks did.

It is sometimes said that the Christian affirmations are unintelligible because in a day when civilization seems to have broken down—seems, indeed, to be about ready to bomb itself out of existence—the concept of a personal God is unacceptable. What these complaints ought more exactly to say is that highly anthropomorphic concepts of God are no longer serviceable and more adequate ones are needed. And no doubt philosophers should labor to perfect a statement about God that will shake off as far as possible the odors of anthropomorphism. But this observation is poorly served by phrases about the inadmissibility of the notion of a personal God, since the notion of an *impersonal* God is simply contradictory. A god neither knowing nor loving (albeit in a manner beyond our imagining) would be inferior to men and hence, by definition, not-god.

Of course, all our concepts of and names for God are scaffoldings of human thought that stand between us and the Divine, even while making it possible for us to think and speak about the One Martin Buber liked to call the Eternal Thou. So it is hard to see that the concept of God as Ultimate Ground of Being is really much superior to the concept of God-out-there. The first makes us better aware of the divine immanence; the second makes us better aware of the divine transcendence, and neither is adequate. Yet inadequate concepts have often served to bring men into touch with the Holy, although theologians are not on that account dispensed from the effort to purify such concepts.

Moreover, in this whole matter of the contemporary obstacles to belief we should avoid the self-centered presumption that our difficulties are quite unparalleled. No doubt it is fearsome to be living at a time when machines have been developed with the power of obliterating the centers of civilization by intention or by sheer mistake. But modern weaponry and other technology are the work of human minds and hands. Why should we suppose that they create a climate in which religious belief is harder to sustain than it was centuries ago, when people were at the mercy of natural forces neither controlled nor understood by them. Belief has always been a challenge, and we should not think our age unique in finding it so.

Secular humanists, however, are put off not only by the content of Christianity but also by the way believers arrive at their conviction. For these humanists fail to see how affirmations about the invisible or about events two millennia ago can be validated, since these affirmations are not based on data directly sensed. But, in fact, precisely because religious faith is not the term of a scientific demonstration, it is more than merely intellectual assent. It is also a homage of trust and obedience in which the believer commits himself wholly because he judges that it is not only reasonable but right to do so.

A determinedly secular humanist, however, will reject religious interpretations of experience because he admits only knowledge of what may be encountered in the spatiotemporal universe. He thinks the Christian dogmas are poetic myths at best and incredible superstitions at worst. If rationality and decency are ever to prevail, he feels, we must stop supposing that there is any such avenue to truth as religious faith. Christian belief must be rejected, he argues, because it cannot be empirically verified. Moreover, it is often demoralizing, "for men who believe absurdities will commit atrocities." This charge is made most poignantly by those who grew up in a Christian environment but afterward left it. As a boy,

Lord Russell was devout, but when he was about thirty he wrote to Lowes Dickinson:

And often I feel that religion, like the sun, has extinguished the stars of less brilliancy but not less beauty, which shine upon us out of the darkness of a godless universe. The splendour of human life, I feel sure, is greater to those who are not dazzled by the divine radiance; and human comradeship seems to grow more intimate and more tender from the sense that we are all exiles on an inhospitable shore.[16]

Now this short book does not aim to furnish even a sketchy summary of the metaphysical arguments for God's existence or for the credibility of Christianity. It only intends to draw out some of the implications of that faith and to do this in a specialized dimension. But let us not forget that this work of simple exposition is made harder because of the painful discrepancy between what Christians profess and what they often do. Their moral failures quite naturally repel their audience. Those who see the ambiguities in Christian lives are not disposed to listen to a recital of the ideals that should be informing those lives. The Church, said John XXIII as he opened the Second Vatican Council, has known "for more than nineteen centuries a cloud of sorrows." But surely the most bitter of these have been the sins and scandals within the community itself. They have been a tragic reality from the beginning of Christian history and were, indeed, predicted by the Lord, Who made it clear often enough that He was founding a society of penitent believers and not one limited to saints. The Christian people is one called to holiness but frequently residing far from it; a people who believe, but with fluctuations; who are loyal, but not consistently so.

From the outset, therefore, the Christian Church has been inspired by the pure and generous lives of some of its members and betrayed by others. Paul was indignant with the Corinthians because they allowed an ugly distinction between rich and poor to be shockingly plain even when they gathered for the Lord's Supper. The apologetes of the following century used often to insist, in response to calculated calumny, that Christians were not anarchical subverters of Roman law and order. The unknown author of the *Letter to Diognetus,* for instance, said that his brethren obeyed the laws that men made but that their lives were better than those laws. Another Christian writer, Minutius Felix, observed that his people did not orate about great deeds, but lived them. *Non eloquimur magna, sed vivimus.*

Yet those early Christians also knew very well that there were inconsistencies that prejudiced rather than certified their cause. One of their spokesmen, perhaps an early bishop of Rome, acknowledged this with painful clarity. "For when the Gentiles hear from our mouth the oracles of God, they wonder at their beauty and grandeur; afterwards, when they find out that our works are unworthy of the words we speak, they turn from this to blasphemy, saying that it is a myth and a delusion."[17]

Here the experience of the second century is the experience of every century. It is not a question of the malice of someone—a Hitler—who had once been a Catholic, or of those who are Christians only in name because they find it socially useful. It is, rather, that at any point in history many people who seriously consider themselves Christians, whether Catholic or Protestant, are liable to warping pressures from the civilization which they share and sometimes even dominate. No doubt there is considerable accuracy in the basic insight of radical behaviorists like Watson and Skinner, for much of what we do is conditioned by our environment. Christianity insists that persons are capable of free choice, but it also considers the actual fullness of freedom to be a mark of maturity that is developed by time and effort alone. The truly free man or woman transcends many of those conditioning forces in the world; but in all too many cases, the cultural influences that nourish un-Christian attitudes are imperfectly recognized and hence not surmounted.

To the degree that such malign influences prevail, the Church is compromised. It is not immune from such contagions today; and now, as always, some members of the Church are its sharpest critics. We are used to having them tell us that most Christian lives are hypocritical, since they are quite as selfish as those of avowed materialists. And we are accustomed to hearing that although some Catholics may behave devoutly according to their own odd lights, they manifest all the while an inhuman indifference to secular concerns and tragedies. Various solutions are thereupon proposed. In England, for instance, the small group known as the Catholic New Left would like to see the Church denounce the whole of Western bourgeois culture and begin to work actively to establish a social order that would realize those Marxist ideals which are thought to accord with Christianity.

Catholic schools are often cited as instances of the gap between promise and performance; and their failures are, of course, more visible than those of individuals, since the former are more public. When we find Catholic schools resisting an ambiguous culture we are consoled because this is what we hope from them. When they fail to do so, we are saddened but still not justified in concluding that Christianity is itself somehow invalidated. There are aberrations in Christian lives as in all lives. Most Christians in Germany were silent before National Socialism, as most Christians in the United States were silent about legally imposed racial segregation. Neither silence was learned from the Gospel; rather, each betrayed it and manifested the human capacity for ratifying evil if only by passive acquiescence. Even the saints fall short because of this tragic capacity, although they fail least. We can apply here the response of Evelyn Waugh when Nancy Mitford reproached him for rudeness toward a young writer: "How could you be so wicked! I thought you were supposed to be religious." Waugh replied: "You can't imagine how much worse I should be if I were not religious."[18] Any Christian will understand that; he knows Christians are men and therefore sinners who are always likely to distress the Church. But if this were not the case, the Church might doubt itself, since it is supposed to be an assembling of those who have sinned and look for redemption.

This consideration may not eliminate the problem created for the credibility of Christianity by the sins of Christians, but it should diminish it. Perhaps that problem can also be put into perspective by a parallel of sorts. The remorse Christians feel at the scandal of their own failures is not unlike the remorse of a thoughtful American when he realizes how often he and his fellow-citizens compromise the nation and its ideals. On October 21, 1967, Americans might have found themselves mortified both by the Vietnam war and by those demonstrating against it in Washington who carried signs that read: "Where is Oswald when we need him?" Yet they would not on these accounts have surrendered the ideals and the pursuit of justice and peace, of equality and civic responsibility within the framework of democratic constitutional government. So Christians must also work at realizing the ideals they profess, even while recognizing that these have never yet been fully achieved nor ever will be.

Some of these ideals have implications for education, and it is our business in the chapters that follow to spell them out. Education itself is usually thought of as both a process and a product. It is the process of actualizing a person's capacities for intellectual and moral growth; it is the product, or relatively stable condition, reached when that process has ripened into the acquisition of an authentic skill or a mature and steady disposition of character. Like figures with breath and depth, both the process and the product have two dimensions, since each has an individual and a social aspect. Thus educational theorists are always found working with the problem of how best to relate the public and private zones of life. Their dominant ethical orientation, which compels them to reflect on social forms, makes them want to educate; and education is conducted only within a community. It presupposes interpersonal exchanges and is firmly shaped by certain social purposes.

The educational theorist has, therefore, a central concern that can be summed up in two perennial and irreducibly important questions. The first asks about the character of an ideal personal development and how it is linked to and dependent on one's essential ordering to a life of association and partnership with others. The second inquires what kind of community, or complex of communities, will serve as the environment for the education of good men. Aristotle seemed to think that the ideal commonwealth would cultivate the individual's potentiality for metaphysical reflection. This, in turn, would bring him to the stature of the complete man and perfect citizen. Even Rousseau did not propose to remove little Émile from every social context—only from the decadent towns to the bracing company of his tutor, so that he could evolve securely from childish self-love to mature benevolence.

These considerations suggest a plan for the rest of this book and topics for its remaining chapters. We must first try to sum up the Catholic worldview with emphasis on those elements most significant for education. A summary of this kind would be a formidable job even if the writer were a professional theologian, which he is not. It is always difficult to speak of divine things without traducing them, which is why Pascal said that only God can speak well about God. But naturally enough the professional biblical scholars and the theologians do better than the rest of us, and we want to draw on their funds. This, though, is hard to do nowadays because the current epoch of crisis has generated such richness of theological literature that the observer is stupefied by its sheer mass. Some of it is technical, some popular; some is nutritious and some eccentric. But taken as a whole, it constitutes a remarkable deepening of the Church's understanding of itself and its belief. No doubt this is a characteristic benefit of any cataclysmic period. If in the fourth century the whole world groaned to find itself Arian, as Saint Jerome said, still there did emerge from that turmoil a firmer understanding of the Church's central faith in Christ, the Lord.

During World War II the remarkable English Jesuit C. C. Martindale was stranded in Denmark where he had gone just before the war made return travel impossible. To pass part of the time, he kept a diary in which, at one point, he noted the need for devising an entirely new way of presenting Christianity if it were to speak to men of the postwar world. "The clergy will never do this," he wrote, "unless awful disasters and all but extermination come upon us or unless we have a quite miraculous and heroically audacious Pope."[19] John XXIII may have been that pope, but we cannot honestly say, despite all the bustle of the theologians, that we have yet those successful new formulations or have registered gains like those which followed the Arian controversies. We can hope for such gains, however, and curiously enough, the anxieties of the hour are grounds for such hope, for they indicate an awareness of that necessity for rethinking the ways of proclaiming Christianity and of relating its message to mankind's newer secular knowledge. The current flood of theological publication is surely one fruit of this awareness. It also warns anyone who ventures an amateur's résumé of Catholicism that he may be offering an impoverished account because he is drawing on yesterday's theology.

On the one hand, my job here is to say clearly what the Christian must say, given the topic and, on the other, not to assert as Christian teaching what is no more than a theological opinion or a personal bias. Once such a sketch has been roughed out, we can go on to ask in subsequent chapters what the individual and social goals of Catholic education are. Not that these two dimensions are fully distinct in concept, much less separable in fact. We all know that we acquire not only knowledge and values but our very image of ourselves in the course of transactions (to use Dewey's term) with others, beginning with our parents. Since, however, Catholicism demands the conversion of the individual even when society itself cannot be changed, it is not unreasonable to distinguish what the Gospel requires of the individual from what it requires of human societies. In the first century, for instance, Christians could not exert upon the emperor the leverage Gregory VII used a thousand years later—and even he was limited enough. But in any age and no matter what the world is like, the Christian must try to overcome hatred in himself; he must be kind even when he cannot criticize with impunity, much less correct, abuses in the civil society. Those first-century Christians had to put up with a slave society because they could not even imagine overturning and reconstructing it. But it is a precious strength of democracies, however imperfect, that their citizens are free to look critically at the nation and to transcend it sufficiently to be able to measure it by higher norms. A white woman in New Orleans defied the mob boycotting a school that had just enrolled a handful of blacks. "If I had to do it over," she told an observer, "I wouldn't have made this system, but how many people ever have a say about what kind of a world they're going to live in?"[20] Not many, for sure. But this woman's voice reminds us that Christians must always be asking themselves what the Gospel means for human fellowship everywhere. Newman wrote:

In truth, the Church was framed for the express purpose of interfering, or (as irreligious men will say) meddling with the world. It is the plain duty of its members, not only to associate internally but also to develop that internal union in an external warfare with the spirit of evil, whether in Kings' courts or among the mixed multitude; and, if they can do nothing else, at least they can suffer for the truth and remind men of it by inflicting on them the task of persecution.[21]

Of course, the accurate practice of this interference requires not only fortitude but shrewd wisdom. One must not trespass on the due autonomy of secular agencies nor use religious zeal to promote irreligious purposes. Yet political realities are usually complex, and there is always the chance that passion and self-deception will turn worldly interests or prejudices into crusades. On the other hand, the insistent voice of mediocrity advises caution rather than martyrdom, and the voice of civil officialdom warns the Church to stick to the sacristy. In September 1957 a news photo from Nashville showed a balding segregationist picketing a school with a fierce placard in one hand and a Bible in the other. In January 1971 a Portuguese priest was tried for having criticized his country's wars in its overseas territories. (The prosecutor was reported to have said that the post-Vatican II Church was struggling with Marxism for control of the masses and had, in so doing, lost "the prestige of eternal values.") In these cases the lines are drawn clearly enough; sometimes, however, they are not. Also in January 1971, an African bishop in Cameroon was sentenced to life imprisonment for allegedly plotting against the government. Newspaper readers in other places could hardly evaluate the issues, but they sensed that this bishop may well have been caught in the ambiguous currents of tribal rivalries.

Yet the duty Newman underlined imposes itself regardless of whether there are difficulties. For here as everywhere, Christian life calls for a synthesis. There is the first commandment and the second; the need for interior religious experience and the need to conform one's life as a citizen to one's belief as a Christian. Thus it was not remarkable to find the council stressing these two themes: the value of the individual person and the importance of community. In their opening message of October 20, 1962, the bishops put it this way: "As we undertake our work, therefore, we would emphasize whatever concerns the dignity of men, whatever contributes to a genuine community of people."

It is just these two emphases, the individual and the social, which provide the foci for the final chapters here. Those chapters are mainly concerned with locating the goals set by the Gospel for education; but before concluding, we must raise the question of the Catholic school. Raise, not answer. Time alone will discover to us the educational forms of the future. No doubt it is already bringing them to birth, for time, as Augustine said in the *Confessions,* takes no holiday. But our chief aim now will be to discern, however faintly, the ideals those forms must serve.

NOTES

1. See *The* (London) *Times Educational Supplement,* January 14, 1966, p. 106. The unfriendly remark of Robert Lowe about the philosophy of education was also picked up from *The Times Educational Supplement,* whose radio critic quoted it in a column, February 19, 1960, p. 313. Lowe, Viscount Sherbrooke (1811–1892), was a controversial minister for education (vice-president of the committee of council on education) in a Palmerston government during the first half of the 1860s.

2. *Religion* is a word that can be given several meanings and sometimes is even used as the label for a bad product. In that case, religion will be equated with the failures of churchgoers—their sins, the stuffiness of the forms they create, or their simple inanities as symbolized by the advertisement for pearloid plastic boxes shaped like a cross to hold the perfume of those "who want the moral uplift and spiritual enhancement of their religion while grooming." It is in view of such things that we will be urged to anticipate a religiousness Christianity or will be told that there may still be something to the Catholic faith, but not to the Catholic religion. But this is not the only way of defining religion, and since not just theologians but philosophers, sociologists, psychologists, and jurists work up definitions of religion and come at it from different angles, the confusion is greater than it need be. Psychologists may conclude that the religious phenomenon is really quite undefinable. A theologian like Tillich may say that religion is essentially an earnest asking after the meaning of existence, and a philosopher like Dewey will identify religious faith with allegiance to whatever ideals one cherishes. A Supreme Court decision cited "those religions based on a belief in the existence of God, as against those religions founded on different beliefs" *Torcaso* v. *Watkins,* 367 U.S. 495 (1960). And, in fact, when a writer wants to include Buddhism and Hinduism among religions, he will define religion as perception of the world's mysteries

and holiness [cf. Ninian Smart, *The Religious Experience of Mankind* (New York: Scribner, 1969), p. 535].

No doubt each of these positions is intelligible in terms of the author's special interests and presuppositions. But we shall bypass all that here and take *religion* to mean what it has commonly meant since the vernaculars emerged from Latin. Two quite disparate comments will serve to mark that general understanding of the word, although neither is intended as an adequate account of all that religion signifies. In a dissent in a case earlier than the one quoted above, Chief Justice Charles Evans Hughes said: "The essence of religion is belief in a relation to God involving duties superior to those arising from any human relation" *U.S.* v. *Macintosh,* 283 U.S. 633–634 (1931). Edmund Wilson, himself an agnostic, was equally direct because of his concern for language itself: "Religion is the cult of a god, or gods, conceived in supernatural terms. The 'religion of humanity' and the 'religion of art' are not religions at all, and it confuses the whole question of religion seriously to use such phrases" [*A Piece of My Mind: Reflections at Sixty* (New York: Farrar, Straus and Cudahy, 1956), p. 3].

Religion will, then, be taken here as it is most commonly taken; that is, to denote the whole zone of man's relationship *and response* to the transtemporal, to the holy, to the divine—to God. When fully developed or "institutionalized," as it is in Catholic Christianity, religion will include a faith or creed, a moral code and a liturgical and sacramental life that serves as a preeminent medium for contact with the divine. Ralph Barton Perry said that for the elder Henry James religion was a matter of insight and experience rather than dogma or historical revelation. But Catholic Christianity is, in fact, both.

3. For good accounts of what philosophy of education is or might be, see Harry S. Broudy, "How Philosophical Can Philosophy of Education Be?" *The Journal of Philosophy,* 52 (1955), 612–622, and R. S. Peters, "The Philosophy of Education," in J. W. Tibble, ed., *The Study of Education* (London: Routledge & Kegan Paul, 1966), pp. 59–89.

4. Sidney Hook, "The Scope of Philosophy of Education," *Harvard Educational Review,* 26 (1956), 148. The comment from *Time* appears in 83 (January 17, 1964), 72.

5. Jacques Barzun, *The American University: How It Runs, Where It Is Going* (New York: Harper & Row, 1968), n., p. 282.

6. Christopher Dawson, *Understanding Europe* (New York: Sheed and Ward, 1952), p. 242.

7. Charles A. Reich, *The Greening of America* (New York: Random Hause, 1970), and Jean-François Revel, *Without Marx or Jesus: The New American Revolution Has Begun,* trans. J. F. Bernard (Garden City, N.Y.: Doubleday, 1971).

8. See the extract from *Petri Abaelardi Historia Calamitatum* in Lynn

Thorndike, ed., *University Records and Life in the Middle Ages* (New York: Columbia University Press, 1944), p. 6.

9. See the translation of the *Epistle of Ignatius to the Philadelphians*, c. 4, which is included in the series of *The Ante-Nicene Fathers*, I, 81. The 1885 American edition of this series, which was first published in Edinburgh in 1867, was reprinted by the Wm. B. Eerdman Company, Grand Rapids, Mich., in 1953.

10. Quoted from the essay, *"Esquisse d'un Univers personnel"* by Henri de Lubac, *The Religion of Teilhard de Chardin,* trans. René Hague (New York: Desclee, 1967), p. 151.

11. "Pastoral Constitution on the Church in the Modern World," *The Documents of Vatican II,* English trans., Walter M. Abbott, S.J., gen. ed. (New York: Guild-America-Association Presses, 1966), n. 33, p. 232.

12. Edith Oliver, *The New Yorker,* 45 (October 25, 1969), 142.

13. Note, though, the wise observation of Quentin Lauer, S.J., who points out that the experience of the greatest philosophers, like that of great artists or religious geniuses, is of exceptional profundity, "a sort of witness to the capacity of human experience at its best." *Hegel's Idea of Philosophy* (New York: Fordham University Press, 1971), p. 10.

14. Charles S. Peirce, "Logic of Mathematics in Relation to Education," quoted from *Educational Review* (1898) in Philip P. Wiener, ed., *Charles S. Peirce: Selected Writings* (*Values in a Universe of Chance*) (New York: Dover, 1966), p. 341.

15. See Edmund Wilson, *A Prelude: Landscapes, Characters and Conversations from the Earlier Years of My Life* (New York: Farrar, Straus and Giroux, 1967), p. 78.

16. Bertrand Russell, *The Autobiography of Bertrand Russell: 1872–1914.* (Boston: Little, Brown, 1967), p. 286.

17. "The So-Called Second Epistle of St. Clement to the Corinthians," n. 13, trans. Francis X. Glimm, *The Fathers of the Church: The Apostolic Fathers* (New York: Cima, 1947), p. 73.

18. From the transcript of a broadcast, "Evelyn Waugh—A Brief Life, Narrated by Christopher Sykes," *The Listener,* 78 (August 24, 1967), 229.

19. Quoted by Philip Caraman, *C. C. Martindale* (London: Longmans, 1967), p. 217.

20. Quoted by Robert Coles, *Children of Crisis: A Study of Courage and Fear* (Boston: Little, Brown, 1967), p. 14.

21. John Henry Cardinal Newman, *The Arians of the Fourth Century,* new ed. (London: Longmans, 1895), Part II, chapter III, section II, pp. 258–259.

3

On the Proclamation of Life in the World to Come: Some Aspects of Catholicism

> It is my Father's will that whoever sees the Son
> and believes in him shall have eternal life.
>
> *John 6:40*

This chapter aims at responding to the plain fact that before saying something about what Catholicism means for education, we must try to say something about Catholicism itself. It does not propose to summarize Catholic belief, however; good books that do this are available, and a thumbnail compendium here would be only a mischievous caricature. Our intentions are, therefore, quite circumscribed. First we make a few observations about ways of studying Catholicism, and then we discuss certain of the general characteristics the faith displays when looked at in the round as a worldview. Of course, this approach involves touching on some of the principal tenets of Christianity and the moral attitudes these should generate. It is not our purpose, however, to expound systematically all the teachings of Catholic Christianity or to defend any of them; we wish only to suggest how, for those who accept this perspective, human existence is made intelligible. This should provide some framework for indicating later on how the Gospel throws light on the aims of education.

WAYS OF STUDYING CATHOLICISM

If the narrow focus adopted here were not imposed by the scope of a small book, it might well be dictated by prudence. No one can hope to produce a fully sufficient account of Christianity in which every essential element is fairly represented and properly balanced with all the others while the whole portrait, without any betrayal of its subject, is still effectively adapted to the mind and taste of the author's contemporaries. We are not surprised to discover that the God of biblical faith, Who must be understood as Absolute or entirely free of any limitation or dependence on others, is most inadequately represented by even highly sophisticated human concepts. For all our notions are colored by our own limiting situation in time and space. But we also learn soon enough that we never fully know even the petty objects with which we interact in the everyday world. In our knowing, we do not create this world but encounter it. If the case were otherwise, we could predict the response of strangers we meet instead of having to await it. To be sure, once I have seen or stumbled over a certain object, I judge it to be a chair. Yet how little of what might be known about it do I actually comprehend, for I have no idea of the nature of its materials, nor who made it, nor how nor why, when or where.

Since it is so difficult to work up a reasonably full understanding of unimportant objects in the everyday world, how fanciful would be the hope of distilling even a schematic and impressionistic summary from the sheer bulk of Catholicism's tradition and history? After all, the Church is now two millennia old, although not everyone will admit that fact. Some people have remarked, delicately or bluntly, that the Roman Catholic Church should be considered the descendant of a certain medieval institution. We can agree, of course, provided the observation is not meant in an exclusive sense, as though there were an early and basic Christian tradition with which the Church of the thirteenth century had no historical and essential continuity. The Roman Catholic Church of today believes itself to be, certainly, the continuation of that medieval church—but also the continuation of the Carolingian church, the church under Constantine, the church under Nero, and the church that emerged from the Cenacle in Jerusalem. It says that certain affirmations of faith have been forces in constituting this community from the beginning, and it continues today to confess that faith in the One and Only God Who is a Trinity of Persons; in the divinity of Jesus the Christ, Who is authentically God and authentically man; in the liberation of men from the detention of sin through the action of Jesus; in the reality and indispensability of God's favoring assistance, called *grace;* and in the defining of life's ultimate purpose as a union with God through Christ encountered in His church, a union designed to lead to eternal life in an Age-to-

Come. Small wonder, then, that a whole bookshelf can not contain an exhaustive and truly definitive statement of Catholic Christianity, even when the subject is examined from the deliberately limited prospect of the professional student of religion.

For Catholicism can, of course, be described from different viewpoints and can be looked at from within or from without. The historian may chronicle its career much as he would that of any other institution and movement met with in the world, although here he is studying the history of a religious society or church. The sociologists and psychologists may deliver descriptive analyses of the actual experiences and attitudes, including the ambiguous ones, of members of that society so that we can know, so to speak, how it feels to be a Catholic. The philosopher of religion may bring his distinctive tools and methods of investigation to bear on these same experiences and attitudes in order to provide a philosophical interpretation of Catholicism as an actuality in the real world.

There is no reason why the practitioners of these disciplines might not be Catholics; however, the disciplines themselves do not require such participation. Moreover, their characteristic procedures and substance differ essentially from those of Catholic theology, which is, in the first place, an effort to expound the message that God is believed to have communicated through the history of Israel and above all in the person and life of Jesus. This theological effort has been under way ever since the first-century Christians began to develop the *didache,* or traditional teaching, which aimed to set forth and interpret the *kerugma,* or proclamation of the central facts about the life and work, the death and resurrection of the Lord.[2] Theology of this kind is normally the province of a believer, and the nature of his job is suggested by these words of one of the most distinguished Catholic theologians of our time:

. . . I have spoken as a theologian. And is it not necessary, when the seriousness of the hour requires it, that the theologian know how to suspend for a moment his historical studies or his personal constructions—to which he would be wrong to attach an exaggerated importance—to recall that his entire existence as a theologian and all the authority that his profession gives him are rooted in the task that he has received: the defense and the explanation of the faith of the church?[3]

But the very fact that the Church now possesses a fund of nearly two thousand years of accumulated theological thought means that it also possesses a rich variety of descriptions of itself and its life and belief. Since these descriptions were developed at various times and from disparate standpoints, they often differ considerably from one another, even when they are dealing with the same matters. Such differences are quite natural characteristics of the human condition. Students of the sociology of knowledge have alerted us to these divergencies in perspective, and the fable of the blind men examining the elephant is a folkloric underscoring of the same point.

Nowadays, everyone is aware that the social life we share has a good deal to do with the way we look at the world and the concepts we form of it. Still, we can recognize as much without proceeding to the extreme conclusion that all concepts are merely the products of a particular cultural setting and the particular mental sets it has nurtured. Indeed, if Karl Mannheim advised his readers not to ignore the social conditioning of thought, he also warned them against supposing that an idea has been adequately explained by the simplistic dodge of labeling it feudal or bourgeois, liberal or conservative. Certainly there are meanings that can survive the passage from one civilization to another. We need not have lived in Homeric Greece to understand the tears of Achilles mourning Patroclus nor in first-century Israel to understand what is meant by a Virgin Birth. A commentator may side with Plato in finding Achilles' grief deplorably excessive, or he may judge the Virgin Birth an odd myth; but he ought not claim that the concepts themselves are incomprehensible to twentieth-century minds.

Like the rest of us, the contemporary theologian has profited from the lessons of this sociology of knowledge. He is critically aware of how differently such themes as the nature of the Church or of faith will present themselves to Christians living at different epochs. But once equipped with the awareness, he may proceed according to his own preferences to stress either the diversities or the agreements between, let us say, the concept of the church in the Pauline letters and in the decrees of Vatican I, or between the nature of faith as propounded by Scholasticism and as propounded by Existential theologians today. For instance, he might begin by noting that Saint Thomas Aquinas spoke of faith precisely as enlarging and informing the intelligence and said that its object is the First Truth, God, even as the object of the physician's art is health. But the writer may then conclude that this Thomistic concept is too one-sidedly intellectual and that it fails to bring out sufficiently the character of faith as a total commitment of the entire person to God in Christ. Still, he could have chosen to emphasize the insight of Thomas's intellectualism, for intelligence is a prime and indispensable vehicle for effecting precisely that gathering up and deliverance of oneself in a distinctively human homage of love and trust. This remains true even though intelligence is not the only power involved in the profound gesture that necessarily synthesizes the head and the heart.

In any case, it is wise to be on the lookout for the displacements of meaning and emphases beneath people's usage of the same terms—otherwise, we may find ourselves talking past rather than to one another.[4] Moreover, the professional theologians and historians of dogma will want an exact knowledge of variations among modes of theological inquiry and their consequent formulations from Augustine's fifth-century North Africa through Aquinas' Paris and Luther's Renaissance Germany to Kierkegaard's Copenhagen and the wide world theologians know today. But the purposes of this book require something more. We must say that we can identify certain principal elements that are basic to the faith of Catholic Christians at all times and in all places, howsoever diversely conceptualized and howsoever badly realized in practice.

A sketch compounded from these elements no doubt would be rudimentary, but it need not be a travesty. It is obvious that a comprehensive and technical survey of all the chief aspects of Catholicism, charting their historical evolution and indicating their precise relationships to the nucleus of the faith, would call for learning, skills, and space quite lacking here. But these deficiencies can be put up with, since our aim is much less ambitious. In fact, the faith of a Christian would itself suggest that this aim is feasible. Just because he believes in Divine Providence, a Christian is confident that he can give some account of his belief. Even though he has not screened each term through the mesh of language analysis, he trusts that his words retain some sense beyond his own historical context. After all, the basic fact in the report that Washington wintered in Valley Forge can be grasped today as well as in 1777, although we may not appreciate it as intensely as the Continentals did. Now the Christian believes that certain events did indeed happen in Galilee and Judea twenty centuries ago and that the results are incomparably real and relevant for the life of all men today because God invites them all to respond to these realities. It must be possible, therefore, to proclaim the Gospel in a fashion that renders it generally intelligible. For it is not to be supposed that God calls only the learned or the exceptionally gifted to a knowledge of these facts and their interpretation. Rather, it is the Christian conviction that He calls everyone and uses each generation of believers to recruit the next. This may well require that the message be freshly formulated; but it also requires that its substance be retained so that the essential Gospel is passed like a torch from hand to hand, although the understanding of that Gospel may expand over the centuries just as a flame may grow stronger.

The Second Vatican Council, speaking of the so-called Eastern Churches (those, for instance, of Constantinople, Antioch, Alexandria, Moscow, Serbia, Greece, Cyprus, and Bulgaria) noted that these had preserved the "basic dogmas of the Christian faith concerning the Trinity and God's Word made flesh of the Virgin Mary." But it went on to add: "However, the heritage handed down by the apostles was received in different forms and ways, so that from the very beginnings of the Church it has had a varied development in various places, thanks to a similar variety of natural gifts and conditions of life."[5] This is the theme we should like to echo: that the basic dogma can be acknowledged even when it is expressed in different forms. The existence of God is affirmed whether we speak of Pure Act or the Ground of Being; His authorship of all things is affirmed whether we call Him Almighty Father or Lord of human history.

It is not surprising, then, to find that thoughtful Christians manifest a significant measure of agreement about what Christianity means and is, even when they speak out of very different traditions and use different rhetorics. This can be illustrated by certain parallels between the thought of two twentieth-century men, C. S. Lewis and Pierre Teilhard de Chardin. Each one did a good deal to lead others to Christianity, although at first sight the pair seem to have had little else in common. The Englishman was inclined to highlight poignantly man's pilgrim condition in this life and the disparity between things of time and the unimaginable, transtemporal fulfillment to which Christians believe the transcendent God summons humanity. Lewis was, therefore, predictably impatient with some of the master themes of Teilhard, who stressed the human vocation to develop the earth, often throwing off exuberant and somewhat ambiguous statements about believing in the future of the universe and discovering "a new face of God: the evolutive God of cosmogenesis." This emphasis quite disenchanted Lewis, and he wrote to a correspondent: "I am entirely on the side of your society for shutting de Chardin up. . . . I can't for the life of me see his merit."[6]

Yet if we look beneath these contrasting surfaces, we find key identities of fundamental conviction and attitude between the great Anglican don and the French Jesuit paleontologist. Their moral likeness is plain enough. Both were endlessly selfless in helping others. But this ethical attitude issued from a common religious outlook. Lewis's noble career (in which he was equally effective in scholarship, in imaginative writing for children and adults, and in popular apologetics) perfectly exemplified Teilhard's ideal of manifesting for others the "Christic" dimensions of life in this universe. On the other hand, Père de Lubac, perhaps the most distinguished commentator on Teilhard's thought, tells us that the first of its three main lines of force is precisely its eschatological character—that is to say, that Teilhard's "eyes are constantly fixed on the ultimate consummation."[7] In short, C. S. Lewis was as much penetrated by loyalty to man's earthly vocation as Teilhard was penetrated by the conviction that "our homeland is in heaven" (Philippians 3:20). We could say of each one what the Archbishop of Canterbury said of John XXIII: "Of all the lessons which he has left, none is more significant than that the deepest humanity and the supernatural go together. His breadth of sympathy and his practical concern were rooted in an utterly other-worldly devotion to God, and he served this world by reflecting in it the light of another."[8]

History offers many such cases of convergences-amid-contrasts. They all remind us that along with the expected pluralism of individual viewpoints and emphases found among Christians speaking of their faith, there is also an underlying unity that is derived from their responding to the same divine Word and trying to reflect it faithfully. We are confident, therefore, that in these pages we can concentrate on certain themes that are truly focal in the belief of Catholic Christians. But that is not to say that the unoriginal profile roughed out in this fashion comes within hailing distance of the previously listed professional approaches, secular or theological, to the study of Catholicism. Ours is much too fragmentary a résumé to be labeled "theology," and it intends the tone of an ordinary guide rather than that of an apologete or an evangelist. There is no attempt here to argue the credibility of these ideas, although there is considerable temptation to try, since we know that the Christian creed strikes a good many people as no more than the relic of prescientific culture. Indeed, some philosophers of language advise us that these religious propositions are not only unwarranted but meaningless because they speak of realities defined as lying beyond the range of human sense experience. The statements embodying them, since they cannot be empirically tested, are therefore said to be strictly nonsensical.[9]

In other words, sometimes it is not just Christianity that is judged unbelievable—the very possibility of any intellectually respectable religious faith is rejected. This refusal is understandable, because in believing, Christians do seem to run counter to the ordinary ways of judging and acting. They say that they *know* certain truths about the nature of things and that this knowledge requires behavior conformed to it. But if they are asked for the evidence that generated the knowledge in question, they reply readily enough that they have no direct evidence demonstrating this reality. Instead, they say that they have accepted this vision on the word of a Person they trust—Jesus, Who is professed to be the Word of God, the Eternal Son Himself.

Now it is certainly not uncommon for men and women to accept the word of another, if they are reassured by their knowledge either of the witness himself or of the circumstances surrounding his testimony. A father believes the son whose candor and decency have never disappointed him. The judge believes the prisoner's admission of burglary if there is no suspicion of coercion, since men do not normally accuse themselves falsely. But the faith of the Christian is something else again. Here the believer does not believe because he exercises an independent check on the witness, but simply because it is God Who testifies. Yet the Christian has never seen God, and it is two thousand years since Jesus preached in Galilee. The paradox, if not scandal, posed by faith suggests that we ought stop over it for a moment.

FAITH AND OTHER
WAYS OF KNOWING

Like any other phenomenon, faith can be approached from different sides.[10] In accord with our interest here in education, we might start with the Christian conviction that faith is, among other things, a way of knowing. This immediately implies that human cognition is pluralistic and proceeds along several very different avenues— and education ought to acknowledge and cultivate them all. Indeed, Vatican II restated this explicit Catholic position by echoing Vatican I of a century before. In the 1965 document on the "Church in the Modern World," the bishops wanted to affirm the legitimate autonomy of human culture, especially the sciences. That autonomy rests on these disciplines having their own laws and values. This, in turn, follows from the very existence, as the earlier council had noted, of " 'two orders of knowledge' which are distinct, namely, faith and reason."[11]

This conviction is clearly important when it comes to determining the scope and goals of a fully human education of intelligence. Its significance may be anticipated if we digress for a moment to indicate how Scholastic philosophy analyzed "reason" itself. Scholasticism, it will be recalled, is a form of Theistic Realism and an intellectual tradition established by medieval thinkers; until very recently, it continued to be influential in a multiplicity of forms, some of them quite diluted. For instance, there were Protestant

Scholastics for several centuries after Luther, and among Catholics the various schools of Scholasticism, particularly Thomism, dominated philosophical work until World War II.

When the Scholastic thinker studied human knowledge, however, his conclusions were not exceptional. Broadly speaking, they were continuous with the classical Greek tradition and they were the ones that most people would ratify from their own experience. Scholasticism taught that even our natural cognitive approach to the world is pluralistic, distinguishing two chief sources of this natural knowledge—the intelligence and the variety of powers that are lumped together under the term "sense." In good practical fashion, for instance, Saint Thomas Aquinas, the most celebrated of the Scholastics, attached great importance to sense experience precisely as our way of having immediate conjunction with reality. Indeed, he described *experience* as the knowing of individual objects through the senses. He also remarked that the existence of things other than ourselves can be known if they fall directly under our senses or if their existence can be inferred from sense data, as when we surmise that where we see smoke, there is a fire.[12] Or we might add, recalling what Paul told the Romans, as when we see God's everlasting power and deity, invisible though they are, manifested in the world He has made.

But although Saint Thomas emphasized the necessity of sense experience for the life of reason, he did not think that sensation is the only kind of cognition and he would have firmly rejected the notions that intellection is simply a matter of shuffling and regrouping sense images and that mind is no more than a special aspect of the body. His own theory of knowledge was designed, therefore, to explain how it is that intellection penetrates more deeply than the senses are capable of doing into the sense data in order to grasp intelligible or transsensible aspects of reality that are imbedded or somehow implied in these data but beyond the reach of the senses themselves.

Through his senses, which are indeed bodily powers, a man knows individual, singular objects of a material nature—the color and scent of this rose. But through his mind, which is itself human but immaterial, he grasps "universal" aspects. These can be applied to many specific instances because, in the process of intellection, they have been liberated from the concrete materiality that ties them down to one particular or another. Thus we have an idea of a rose or a man which expresses, although not completely, the true nature of the thing. These concepts can, therefore, be predicated of many roses or many men. It is in such predications, moreover, that truth is formally reached. However, although the process that culminates in this predication has a certain freedom from sense experience, it still begins with that sense-awareness. One of Saint Thomas's virtuoso metaphysical performances is a subtle theory devised to explain how this intellectual knowledge arises out of the interpenetrating action of senses and intelligence, body and spirit.

Even if we do not find such theories persuasive, most of us will agree that we have a capacity for knowing and that it is many-stranded. This capacity includes not only seeing and hearing but also such diverse functionings of intelligence as immediately apprehending patterns of intelligibility in single cases (as when a baby indignantly recognizes, while his mother divides a cookie, that a whole is greater than its parts); or mapping out plans for a trip by elaborate reasonings; or getting the point of a joke in an intuitive flash. Now besides these commonly acknowledged sources of knowledge, Christians arrive at convictions about the existence of God and the divinity of Jesus through yet another kind of experience. We should like to point out some of the features of this experience in order to reject two overdrawn oppositions which can distort the concept of faith. The first of these would, as Paul VI put it, so thoroughly separate faith from reason that faith itself would be reduced to the condition of some lower and improper use of intelligence.[13] The other would make of Catholicism a religion of faith in too sharp contradistinction to a religion of experience, whereas in its fullness it is both.

We might start by noting that Catholics consider their faith-life to be the full development of an experience that all adults will have had, at least in germinal form and at some time. For all persons are, to use Karl Rahner's phrase, potentially believers, and all live in a world whose natural dimensions have been enlarged and elevated by a special divine intervention. Christians, and indeed many other religious men, believe that God is present and active everywhere and always in this universe, and that His saving action permeates the histories both of individuals and of societies. The books of the Old Testament announce this conviction that the world is filled with God Whose effects we experience even if we do not see Him. "His glory fills the whole earth (Isaiah 6:3) . . . Do I not fill heaven and earth? (Jeremiah 23:24) . . . The world and all it holds is mine (Psalm 50:12) . . . The Spirit of the Lord, indeed, fills the whole world" (Wisdom 1:7).

But beyond this creativity of God sustaining the cosmos, Christians acknowledge His special action in human lives as He works to draw all persons into the fullness of union with Himself. The rather opaque technical term for this action is *grace.* In its chief document, the "Dogmatic Constitution on the Church," Vatican II spoke of the universality of grace:

His plan was to dignify men with a participation in His own divine life. . . . All men are called to belong to the new People of God. . . . Nor is God Himself far distant from those who in shadows and images seek the unknown God, for it is He who gives to all men life and breath and every other gift (cf. Acts 17:25–28), and who as Savior wills that all men be saved (cf. I Tim. 2:4).[14]

This theme was repeated in the "Pastoral Constitution on the Church in the Modern World." Here, after speaking of the effects on Christian lives of the memory of Christ's life, death, and resurrection, the council added:

All this holds true not only for Christians, but for all men of good will in whose hearts grace works in an unseen way. For, since Christ died for all men, and since the ultimate vocation of man is in fact one, and divine, we ought to believe that the Holy Spirit in a manner known only to God offers to every man the possibility of being associated with this paschal mystery.[15]

That divine action may work through very commonplace experiences as well as through distinctively religious ones. As the great eighteenth-century spiritual writer de Caussade happily put it, the present moment is always a sacrament; that is to say, it is always a sign of the divine purpose and of prevenient invitations from God and His extension of His divine assistance.[16]

And will there not have been in any life some precious experiences in which the divine reality and power were manifested, even if they were neither then nor later clearly recognized? Suppose that in his old age an agnostic looked back in memory over all his years and in Proustian fashion called up all the experiences of the past, all those long lost to consciousness. Would he not recollect some moment in that history when he had experienced, if not an awareness of God breaking in on his life, at least the sense that the religious question was being raised or the conviction that, if he pursued a line of thought far enough, took a certain turning, the religious question would be raised? The bishops at the Second Vatican Council expressed their belief that this does, in fact, usually happen by making this comment: "Man is constantly worked upon by God's Spirit, and hence can never be altogether indifferent to the problems of religion. The experience of past ages proves this, as do numerous indications in our own times. For man will always yearn to know, at least in an obscure way, what is the meaning of his life, of his activity, of his death."[17]

Such "religious" experiences are as numberless as the multitudes of men and women. Some may appeal chiefly to the head, others touch chiefly the heart. A man walking along a deserted beach at dawn and watching the sun rise out of the boundless ocean may well have the intimations of which Saint Paul spoke. For those luminous immensities of sea and sky elevate him almost irresistibly to an affective conviction of, at the very least, "Something beyond"—to use a phrase Dewey employed in a not wholly dissimilar context.[18] Or perhaps upon some very personal occasion of great bewilderment or pressure, one will seem to have an enlightenment and strength quite beyond normal abilities; or he may meet another who provides unforeseen help or embodies a sustaining ideal of goodness and courage that buoys him up and again suggests a Beyond. If a man reflects on these experiences, he is apt to conclude that they have been, by even a minimal reckoning, singular events with singular implications.

But the distinctive experiences that lead people to make an act of faith in Jesus, one which includes committing themselves to this Lord in a spirit of trusting love and obedience, are much more explicit than the events of which we have just spoken. This could be illustrated from the history of a person growing up in a Christian family; it is somewhat clearer, however, in the case of one who is converted to Christianity in adulthood. There are many witnesses here, and even a library of books by converts. Indeed, there are as many routes leading to conversion as there are persons who have taken that step (after an experience that may have been prolonged and complex or as swift as that of Saul on the Damascus road). Taken together, these testimonies demonstrate how various are the signs that conduct people to faith. For in every case the man or woman concerned recognized certain indications in life's happenings suggesting that it would be reasonable to believe and that this ought to be done. Such evidence, to be sure, does not necessitate decision in the same way that the steps of a mathematical demonstration necessitate their conclusion. For if faith were no more than the inescapable termination of a logical process, every good logician would be a Christian. On the other hand, the knowledge of these signs comes to have an inexpressibly profound resonance in the life of the one who reads them. An attractive statement of one such experience was provided by Mary Crozier, a television critic for *The Tablet* of London, after she had watched a program produced by Malcolm Muggeridge.

A personal recollection enables me best to estimate the immediate effect of Malcolm Muggeridge's three films, entitled collectively *A Life of Christ*, which were shown on BBC 2 in Holy Week. I was not brought up in any

Church, and had never read the New Testament, but when I was nineteen I read Matthew and John for the first time, in Greek, in order to pass the then obligatory "Divvers" examination at Oxford. How extraordinary, strange and haunting a story I found this, coming to me with all the freshness of another language; how poignant and penetrating those words of Christ which echo in the heart and will not be shaken off. Anybody thus reading this story for the first time must answer the question: is it true, or is it not true? If it be true, then Christ lives; and if he lives, then I must become a Christian. That was the direct process, and I was strongly reminded of my awakening wonder at that first discovery of the gospels by Muggeridge's pilgrimage to the Holy Land on television. . . . Muggeridge, while sometimes talking like a political observer and making remarks about the Arabs or reflecting on the misuse of power, was visibly and increasingly affected by the pilgrimage he was making. At the end he had found that you do indeed have to ask whether Christ lives and declaring himself "a true child of these troubled times" he testified, as a result of his pilgrimage, that "Christ is alive."[19]

This is instructive testimony because it has both a convincingly personal note and at the same time brings into clear relief the distinctive character of the specifically Christian religious experience. We can see that there had been evoked for Mary Crozier and for Malcolm Muggeridge, whether by reading or by an actual visit to Israel, a vivid sense of Christ's world. This provided an ambience within which their thought encountered Jesus and His message, and the impact was enormous.

In fact, those who do not share this faith will think the impact enormously disproportionate. Naturally speaking, it was, for the Gospel cannot be directly verified by an appeal to sense-experience. (Neither, for that matter, can many of the testimonies we make about ourselves to one another.) Thus to sympathetic observers the phenomenon of faith may suggest that more than ordinary human strengths of mind and heart are involved. Of course, to the hard-headed agnostic logician it may only suggest self-hypnosis; but to make that charge, the agnostic has to indict a good many people as intelligent and quite as hard-headed as himself.

In any case, what we want to note here is that the judgment made by Christian converts is not irrational because it is not unsupported by evidence. Nor is the evidence all strictly private: some of it is objective; that is to say, it flows from the character of the Gospel itself, from the import of happenings therein recounted, and from their subsequent influence on history. The very words of Christ, for example, have an unmatched power and sublimity which answer to the deepest human longings: "If the Son makes you free, you will be free indeed. . . . If anyone believes in me, even though he dies he will live, and whoever lives and believes in me will never die. . . . Do not let your hearts be troubled. Trust in God still, and trust in me. . . . If you know me, you know my Father too" (John 8:36; 11:25–26; 14:1, 7). Then Christ's life and work, above all His crucifixion and resurrection, the supreme sign and miracle which the Christian community unceasingly proclaims, are understood as the credentials of that exalted doctrine. When this Gospel is met, therefore, it often evokes a recognition and response within the hearer which themselves serve as subjective or internal evidences of its credibility.

Of course the significance of such evidence will not impress everyone. However, it can be affirmed that believers are reasonable, for they judge intelligently enough that their experience encloses signs declaring that Christ's word is believable and should be accepted precisely because it is His and because He lives. Therefore, at one and the same time the Christian will accept Christ as the manifestation of God and will accept what He manifests. The profession of faith, consequently, accomplishes an enlargement of his field of vision, of his thought. It was with this in mind that Aquinas, commenting on the Apostles' Creed, made his famous observation that none of the ancient philosophers knew as much about God as, following on the revelation of Christ, one old woman knows by faith. This is logical enough since, as a contemporary theologian has pointed out, believing is always a matter of knowing some reality by sharing the knowledge and consciousness of another person, and Christians are convinced that through their faith they share the mind of Christ.[20]

Some corollaries should be added. It is clear, to begin with, that one is not a Christian if he joins the Church for a purely earthly reason—because everyone else in town does or because he might otherwise have bad luck. Not that such motives cannot exist. Paul complained of those who were preachers of Christ for dishonest reasons (Philippians 1:17). But one is really a Christian because he accepts the Christ presented in the New Testament, and by doing so accepts as well the existence of a God of loving Providence Who promises eternal life to those who strive to live by the Gospel. Then it should be noted that faith in its fullness also involves recognizing and accepting the Church as the community of believers in which Christ is met in a special way because of His unique presence and action there.

From this it follows that religious faith is more than a matter of knowledge and intellectual assent. For people who truly believe draw deeply on those inner resources of love and freedom which, along with consciousness, are the constituents of their own person-hood. Since they have never seen the Lord but have only under-stood the signs prompting them to accept His word just because it is His, the actual commitment made in the profession of faith embodies a homage of trust and obedient love. The life of faith, in its turn, must include the whole affective response to that divine Word and a consistent effort to conform behavior to belief.

Even from so hasty a tour as this, we can see that the Catholic concept of faith, whether we speak of the act of trusting assent or of the life shaped to accord with it, is that of a highly complex phenomenon that is said to be rational and free and yet entirely dependent on the elevation of mind and will by divine assistance. For Catholicism affirms that the very power of responding to God's antecedent invitation to believe as well as the actualization of this power are themselves His gifts. Therefore, faith can be discussed in greater or less detail as we try to assess the proportions of its several components. Faith can simply be pointed to as it is in the unadorned Gospel stories of the disciples' following of Jesus, or it can be made the subject of searching philosophical analyses. These studies can be extended to examine the not uncommon psy-chological experience in which people are conscious that along with faith there coexist in themselves certain leanings toward unbelief that have progressively to be diminished.[21] It will be the knotty task of the professional theologian to construct a workable account of how we are to understand the three aspects of faith—its reasonableness, its liberty, and its dependence on God's grace—as well as their attendant psychic vibrations. Indeed, strictly speaking he cannot hope for a complete explanation because the presence of divine causality means that there is operating in the picture a crucial factor of which he has no direct consciousness.

But the two points that we wished to make here have been, we hope, indicated. The first is that faith in the Catholic tradition in-volves intelligence and is a way to knowledge. It is conceived as the noblest exercise of the mind and does not at all stand in a pos-ture of irrational opposition to reason. In the second place, the life of faith does not abolish but nourishes religious experience, whether this be the experience of God's manifestations of grace within the ordinary texture of existence or the distinctively Chris-tian experience of knowing and loving God in the knowledge and love of Jesus. In these pages we focus more on the content of Christian faith than on the religious experiences it generates; how-ever, we want to affirm the existence of both dimensions.

**A TEACHING AND
A WAY-OF-LIFE**

When Christians speak about their faith, they hope for accuracy, but they need not aim at the objectivity of a camera or tape recorder. For although, as we observed earlier, we do not literally create the world we know, still a certain subjective factor influences our choice of perspective and colors our judgments, without necessarily reducing them to a species of subjectivism or falsifying them. It is useful to recall here the image of human life as a journey, a symbol surely as old as civilization itself. It reminds us that the landscape we cross is seen quite differently early in the morning, at noon, and toward evening; it looks one way from a hill-top and another from alongside the road in the plain. Moreover, our own affective states, whether ups or downs, can heighten our perceptions, as E. M. Forster noted when he described a character as gripped by one of those depressed moods that open on wider, if grayer horizons.

So it will happen that no one sums up his Christian faith and experience in exactly the same way at every point of his life. The angle of vision he chooses today might not have recommended itself twenty years ago. Virginia Woolf said that the novelist must relate the world of his characters to the unseen world of his own values and convictions. No doubt, every thoughtful person tries to achieve a similar unification of his own ideals and experiences. In somewhat the same fashion, we want to relate a view of the ends and means of education to the Catholic universe of values and convictions; we do this because we think the Gospel throws some light on these activities. But since that universe is experienced not as closed but as opening on an infinite expanse, no one grasps it fully in the sense of knowing all it means and all that this meaning implies for action. This is why no general statement about Catholicism can ever be perfectly poised and final.

But all statements will fall below the level of minimal acceptability unless two essentials are kept in focus, no matter what perspective is adopted for looking at them. This is because Catholicism is both a *teaching* about the world and man and their relationship to God and also a *way-of-life* flowing from, informed by, and according with this teaching.[22] The concept of that way-of-life is itself threefold, although in the real order these three strands interpenetrate. There is the moral ideal which Christians must interiorize and on which their living should be consistently modeled. There is the experience of familiarity with God, uniquely encountered in Jesus, both through the inwardness of individual prayer and through the shared public cult. Finally, there is the active, interpersonal communion with and service of others in the family and in civic society as well as in the fellowship of the Church. These three forces should converge to form distinctively Christian minds and hearts.

It is important to recognize this complexity of Catholicism so that distorting oversimplifications can be avoided. For although Christianity does include, as we have been at pains to say, an essential cognitive element, a knowledge through faith, still the Christian life is not a form of Gnosticism in which salvation is achieved principally through knowing. And although every Christian has some religious experiences, still he is not constituted a Christian by even the most precious intuition of the presence of God. He is a Christian if he does the work of a Christian, which is to accept the revelation that is the person and word of Jesus and to shape his whole life by it. Quite to the point here is a line of Thoreau: "At what an expense any valuable work is performed! At the expense of a life."[23]

It is also important to see that these two elements, the teaching and the way, are organically linked. At the level of theory they are related like the halves of a diptych whose full meaning would be lost if either panel were missing; at the level of existence they must be united in the synthesis of the individual Christian's life. Jesus Himself often insisted that His Gospel was a truth to be lived out and not just contemplated. "It is not those who say to me, 'Lord, Lord,' who will enter the kingdom of heaven, but the person who does the will of my Father in heaven (Matthew 7:21) . . . Happier those who hear the word of God and keep it! (Luke 11:28) . . . The man who lives by the truth comes out into the light, so that it may be plainly seen that what he does is done in God" (John 3:21). Moreover, it is precisely by forming his inner and outer life in accord with this Gospel that a man actually comes to know its truth: "My teaching is not from myself: it comes from the one who sent me; and if anyone is prepared to do his will, he will know whether my teaching is from God . . ." (John 7:16–17). Thoughtful Christians have always reminded one another that if they want to know what the Gospel means, they must live by what it requires.

The Gospel, in other words, knows very well of that complex interplay between knowledge and action that has been studied by philosophers from Aristotle through Aquinas to Peirce, James, and Blondel. Indeed, it can be read, as Paul VI said, in the key of action. "Man's worth lies, we could say in the last resort, not so much in what he is, but in what he does" and so "the school of the Gospel, updated in awareness and in methods, tends to make man an activist."[24] Then if there is the right sort of reciprocity, this action in turn will nourish knowledge—which is no surprise. People have always known, whether philosophers acknowledged it or not, that there is a distinctively practical exercise of intelligence in which knowledge is both completed and validated by action. A person discovers whether a chair is comfortable only by sitting in it. The example is trivial, but the principle it exemplifies is highly significant in the moral order. A man is entitled to be called compassionate if he consistently manifests compassion—a rare achievement indeed! And only such a man really understands what compassion is and how much it is to be valued.

The Christian life must embody this kind of vital relationship between knowledge and action, between belief and practice. In fact, moral action is most characteristically Christian precisely when it is the expression of distinctively Christian faith. Of course, this is not to say that most of the specific ethical conclusions subscribed to by Christians are uniquely their own; nor does it imply that a morality has necessarily to be joined to a religious faith. The Greek and Roman moralists taught much the same ethics as Christianity does, and that consensus did not astonish early Christians. Paul had already observed that ever since the world began it has been possible for men to know the fundamental moral law expressed by their own nature.[25] And so, as Henry Chadwick pointed out, when Celsus in the third century complained that Christian ethical teaching was not new, Origen readily agreed. He turned this into an argument for the Gospel on the grounds that it showed that this Gospel was itself "a republication of the law of nature implanted by creation."[26] But in fact, Origen was engaged in a polemicist's overstatement. In line with his apologetic purposes, he minimized two crucial factors in Christian morality: its central motivation and the particular way it makes its moral imperatives concrete and defines their range. It is not the "law of nature" that prompted Mother Teresa to say to her fellow-workers among the dying and totally destitute of Calcutta's streets: "Let the people eat you up."

In real life, Christian morality is essentially different from the philosophical codes because it is understood as the necessary expression of that love of God which must manifest itself in the loving service of one's brethren in humanity. This necessity is derived, in turn, from the action of Christ which has the transcendent significance of a binding example given by the Son of God. It is precisely because Christ led a life of selfless service that a Christian is obliged to aspire toward being, in Bonhoeffer's celebrated phrase, a "man for others." Christians may fail to fulfill this obligation, but they cannot substitute a human alternative for this divine exemplar.

No doubt, a somewhat similar ideal could be made to rest on a naturalistic basis, for moral philosophers have often proposed the moderating of egoism by a concern for others. But for the Christian, who derives his inspiration and motivation from a person, not from a theory, this model is beyond debate, since it is not at all like that of Socrates or Gandhi. It is important to mark the difference between philosophies and Christianity in this matter of the reasons advanced for altruism and the extent to which we propose to carry this altruism. Otherwise we stumble into that crude ethical simplism which flattens out essential differences and might even reduce to the one category of hedonism those who seek happiness through self-centered gratification and those who who seek it by relatively selfless service of others. In moral matters, both the motives and the circumstances enter into the makeup of good action and, since a gesture that is noble in itself can be corrupted by evil intent or by the wrong setting, both motives and circumstances must be taken into account. Christian altruism, for instance, is obliged to be universal in scope. It must reach even to its enemies, regardless of whether psychiatry judges this impossible. Indeed, Isocrates in Athens, four centuries before Christ, remarked that the man of worthy character will judge it disgraceful to be surpassed by his friends in doing kindnesses. But he added: or by his enemies in doing injury.

The First Letter of John argues that knowing God and keeping His commandment are identical, since to refuse obedience would be to repudiate that special awareness which is part of the friendship with God about which John is writing. The commandment in question is preeminently a summons to believers to build a beloved community through responsible generosity toward one another. We perceive, then, the following line of thought: To believe in and love Jesus is to know and love God. To know and love God is to keep His commandment. To keep His commandment is to live for others as Jesus did, since He told His followers to love one another just as He had loved them—unto death. Christ, as Paul reminded the Philippians, looked not to His own interests but to those of others; and Christians are to have that same mind in themselves. This is the conviction Cesar Chavez voiced so movingly when, at the end of his long fast for the farm workers' cause he said: "It is my deepest belief that only by giving our lives do we find life. . . . To be a man is to suffer for others. God help us be men."[27]

We note this matter of Christian morality precisely because so much educational theory is really a kind of moral philosophy, judging what education should be in light of what its author thinks goodness is. Many people, to be sure, deplore the least association of morality with religion. But for Christians, the bond between their ideals of behavior and their faith is so substantial that to consider the one without the other would be a hopeless mutilation.

Certainly other moral systems have developed apart from religion. The ethics of Confucius and the ethics of the Graeco-Roman moralists were as independent in this respect as that of John Dewey. Indeed, more so. For John Dewey's great ideal of the democratic society was surely derived in part from his devoutly Protestant family and from the civic milieu of his Vermont boyhood. He seemed, in fact, to have recognized this himself. There are well-attested reports of his having remarked, while traveling in the Orient, that he had come to see that certain ways of acting which he had once assumed were products of normally decent human impulses were really the fruits of the Christian outlook.[28] His own ideal of service might well have been one case in point. For the ideal of service is characteristically Christian and alien to the spirit of the Oriental kingdoms and ancient Greece and Rome. In those environments, service was something given by a slave and not at all the aspiration of men who were rich or wise or free. It became the beacon for such men also when a voice was heard to say: "For the Son of Man himself did not come to be served but to serve, and to give his life as a ransom for many" (Mark 10:45).

It is beyond our power to settle the final question of whether it is possible to be faithful in practice to the full Christian ethic without subscribing to the Christian dogma, or, conversely, really to believe the dogma without trying to live by the ethic. But to say the least and the most, it appears doubtful. Those seventeenth-century princes, Catholic and Protestant, who allowed prisoners to be broken to death on the wheel strike us as hardly Christian at all, even when we are told that in a brutal age, order had to be maintained by terror, and even though we know, as E. L. Mascall noted, that human freedom allows people to believe in one thing and do another.[29]

We are still inclined to conclude that since Christianity is not a matter of detached and merely speculative knowing, Christian belief will not be vital when the Christian imperatives of kindness and mercy dwindle so far out of sight. On the other hand, we have often enough seen the Christian ethic wither away once it has been uprooted from the soil of Christian dogma. In any case, Christians must believe that God alone scrutinizes hearts and that it is not for them to decide these issues. For our purposes, it suffices to acknowledge the indispensability both of the dogma and the ethic and to note the bond between them. Each is significant for educational theory, since all such theories are largely statements about the moral and intellectual goals of education in terms of one's understanding of man, his universe, and his destiny.

THE RELEVANCE OF
THE CHRISTIAN OUTLOOK

No doubt, Christianity has something to say about human nature and therefore has some implications for education. But what of it? *Are* these implications at all relevant? Must we not acknowledge the fairly widespread conviction that no reasonably traditional presentation of Christianity can expect to be received in contemporary secularized civilization? For this culture is said to find the Christian doctrine irrelevant, if not meaningless, preferring theories of morality having no significant ties to religion. As a generalization, that analysis may be accurate enough. At least, it is agreed to by distinguished theologians and by distinguished behaviorists, by Karl Rahner on the one hand and B. F. Skinner on the other. We have all heard, indeed rather too often, that the marvelous technological flowering of the last four centuries has not only made it possible to place men on the moon but has also persuaded us that now we really control both our natural and social environments—or we could, if we would. The idea of a creating and providential God is expendable, since we can explain what occurs within the cosmos in terms of that system itself. In fact, religious belief is actually an impediment to the building of a future that will be worthy of humanity because it will take man himself for its ultimate goal. (By a nice paradox, though, some of the American astronauts have made explicit avowals of Christian faith while spinning around in space or standing on the moon.)

But without denying either the stunning victories of technology or the ascendancy of such nontheistic humanisms as those of Marx or American Naturalism, we might still enter some qualifications against these received generalizations. This can be done without reviving that romanticism which hankers for the days when men's own bodies were their chief machines, when human labor was brutalizing and its outcome chancy. The elimination of much of that gross physical pressure is surely a major blessing of machine technology, as even the most determined admirer of homespun and agrarianism must admit. But is there not another side to this coin? And is it so clear, after all, that contemporary man controls his universe?[30] We are not thinking of the fact that now and then the Mississippi floods several states, that a tornado in Kansas can level a college campus within minutes, or that we still experience economic depressions. The real ground for doubting those famous claims is that the advance of technology has itself been darkened by serious ambiguities; indeed, it appears to be destroying the natural environment as well as diminishing the quality of human life in some new ways. It is true that without modern technology Japan could not have wonderfully rebuilt itself after 1945; still, the shadows left by vaporized bodies on ruined walls in Hiroshima remind us that the machine can serve not only to master the world but to end it. To be sure, it is not the machine itself that should be questioned, but simply the thesis that scientific and mechanical developments now justify the comfortable feeling that mankind is securely in charge here.

And then we also wonder just how widespread such feelings really are. For instance, is the loss of interest in the question of God worldwide or largely typical of the urbanized peoples of the Atlantic community? Even among the nations of that community, are there not marked differences from one to another as well as among the subgroups that constitute each of them? It is no surprise to learn that interest in religion is mild among the older members of university milieux. Moreover, the English author of a book called *The Humanist-Christian Frontier* reported that in his country "the man in the street finds Christianity beautiful, unconvincing and irrelevant. He is vaguely agnostic and humanistic in outlook. . . ."[31]

Maybe so. But it would be rash to form similar judgments about the United States, which is much larger, encompassing many widely different regions and being capable of volatile changes in religious enthusiasm. The day before yesterday, in the 1950s, we were swept along by a religious revival. Although church membership is not an automatic guarantee of authentic faith, still it is noteworthy that 60 percent of all our citizens were then professing such membership—and the librarian in Kilgore, Texas, reported that more religious books were stolen than any other sort. Yesterday, by contrast, the "death of God" was a chic theme, and we were being told that most of those church memberships were dreadfully equivocal.

But as the 1970s opened, two graduate students were writing in the *Yale Alumni Magazine:* "Most of today's students are not hostile to a minister's attempt to reveal meaning. Just 10 years ago students were often smug atheists or despairing existentialists. But things are different today. Students welcome new ideals—even mysterious ones."[32] A moving, if exotic, manifestation of this flowering of religion among the young is seen in those little groups that combined a hippie style with a deep devotion to Christ. Their theology is rather fundamentalistic, and they avoid the established church in favor of their own small evangelical communities. But one can admire the fervor of these "Jesus freaks" (the term of their detractors, which they willingly appropriate) and their charity toward anguished people on the edge of society.

It can be objected, of course, that such tiny, colorful outcroppings hardly characterize the national religious landscape. And indeed, if our novelists and dramatists really speak of and for the majority, then American civilization is a vast spiritual desert peopled by hollow men, from the inner cities to outer suburbia, and from the Bronx's Grand Concourse through the villages of Indiana to Laguna Beach. Yet one is not entirely convinced. The artist's picture may be exact enough, but how representative is it? Can we safely intuit a general conclusion from these particulars? Is the indictment true of all or even of most people? Is it even true of anyone all the time, given that even the most commonplace life is far too mysterious for the most subtle art perfectly to encompass. Since, as Gide remarked, it is hard to make great literature out of noble sentiments, most writers select fairly plump targets. It is much easier to give one's work momentum by concentrating on the darkest side of bizarre characters in a desperate fix. Meanwhile, the middle class remains largely a class of believers despite all the ambiguities, and there are moving evidences of religious depth among the poor. Robert Coles has written of the humbling manifestations of faith he met among black sharecroppers, white tenant farmers, migrants, and the mountain people of Appalachia. "I kneel all week long with the beans, but on Sunday I kneel to speak with God. . . ."[33]

These instances are cited not to demonstrate a conclusion but to point toward a caution. They suggest some reason to distrust those confident generalizations which announce that religion has finally run down altogether and is presently visible only under glass in the museums of the city, which is not just secular but triumphantly secularizing. Toward the close of his masterful study of the philosophy of religion, James Collins warned his readers against mistakenly presuming that now "man's religious tendencies have been caught up into a condition of *stasis*."[34] His own reflections persuaded him that this was not so, and the ordinary observer is likely to agree. There is evidence that religion is still a force that focuses, organizes, and gives meaning to the lives of many people. Let us, then, conclude by briefly indicating one of the ways in which Catholic Christianity does this for its adherents.

THE PROCLAMATION OF LIFE IN THE WORLD TO COME

At this mention of rising from the dead, some of them burst out laughing; others said, "We would like to hear you talk about this again."

Acts 17; 32

If we encircle the enormous topic of Christian belief, we discover many angles from which it can be viewed—it is not claimed that the perspective adopted here is the only possible one or even the best one. We simply propose that the Gospel message can be seen as proclamation of the answer to life's ultimate problem, which is that of its own mortality. Nearly everyone will agree that death is just what Saint Paul called it—the final enemy, which neither philosophy nor science has yet been able to put down. But as long as this is the case, any theory of life itself remains incomplete, like an unresolved series of chords, because the transitory character of all earthly things prevents us from finding in them any absolute meaning, goodness, or happiness. Whitehead was only putting gracefully a common realization when he said: "The ultimate evil in the temporal world is deeper than any specific evil. It lies in the fact that the past fades, that time is a 'perpetual perishing.' "[35] And perhaps he was thinking of this perishable quality when he noted elsewhere that the religion that would succeed would be the one "which can render clear to popular understanding some eternal greatness incarnate in the passage of temporal fact."[36]

The observation is compelling, and it reminds us that Christianity does indeed emphasize the crucial importance of earthly life, which can lead to quite another kind of life without end in an Age-to-Come. The common objection to this belief is that it depreciates the value of life in this world. This dissent was roughly phrased by a French actress who said: "I'm a complete agnostic and I don't believe in God. Life after death is bull and the principle that we should live a certain kind of life in one place because it will prepare us for another life somewhere else is ridiculous."[37] We say in the next chapter, however, that Christian faith in an existence beyond time and space does not downgrade the values of time but actually enhances them. Furthermore, since that level of future existence can in no wise be imagined, Paul was already firmly discouraging attempts to fill in its details when he told the Corinthians that these things are beyond the mind of man and unseen by any eye, unheard by any ear.

Christianity does not say that although our individual selves are forever coming into and going out of existence, our lives have a general abiding significance because the race itself is immortal.

For no answer to the problem of death can really claim to be such unless it also claims that death does not have the last word and that we as distinct persons defeat it. This is what Catholicism confesses to have been affirmed in the words of Christ: "If anyone believes in me, even though he dies he will live, and whoever lives and believes in me will never die" (John 11:25–26).

To single out this one aspect is not to say everything about Christianity; but since death is such a universal concern, it does furnish a good point of entry. Surely there is no one whose life has been so sunny and unreflective that it never echoed, as Auden put it in one of his Marginalia, to "thoughts of his own death, like the distant roll of thunder at a picnic."[38] Nor is it just the old who notice how living is interlaced with dying. A French journalist reported in the late autumn of 1969 that de Gaulle in his retirement was not only completing his memoirs but also meditating on death. This awareness of death impending does not normally surface in the young, for in more tranquil times Hazlitt's comment that no young man ever really believes he will die is probably true. But in the last decades of the twentieth century a vivid sense of the question posed by death has not been limited to colossal aging heroes. It was another reporter, an American this time, who recorded conversations with some seventy ordinary Chicagoans in the 1960s. One of them, a nineteen-year-old from Eastern Kentucky, was talking about the Vietnam war. "As far as going over and dyin', I think every man, even though he's a sinner or a Christian, he looks forward to his judgment. So I figure, if he's in Vietnam, that's his duty, to die."[39] And from Vietnam itself there was an echo of this fatalism in the words attributed to a Vietcong defector: "If I die today, I won't have to die tomorrow."

May we not take it as evident, then, that to be human is to know that oneself will die. It is equally evident that this knowledge cannot be entirely suppressed; indeed, according to some students of personality disorders, even the effort at suppression is harmful. Where, asked Rollo May, "does the anxiety engendered by this repression of death and its symbols go? Into our compulsive preoccupation with sex."[40] But if it is generally agreed that death is the fundamental human problem, there is not the same agreement about the answer to it. Instead, there are two radically different ways of looking at this ultimate fact and two possible images for it. One of these images imposes itself on us naturally and even inevitably. The other has scarcely been dreamt of, much less resolutely affirmed, apart from Christianity. The first is the image of death as night, for death at its easiest seems very much like the ingathering of shadows and the deepening of dusk into night and a falling asleep forever. Sir Winston Churchill was a great man, but he was hardly very clever or original when he said that he thought death only meant entering on "some kind of velvety cool blackness."[41] Left to itself, the most ordinary mind could get that far.

Perhaps most men and women have, at least fleetingly, a faint hope for or intimation of life after death. But their actual experience conducts them, at best, only to an abstract philosophical assertion of immortality. That is why people carrying an exhausting burden of grief sometimes turn to spiritism in search of more specific reassurance. It is also why mankind appears to divide itself, at the deepest level, into two groups. There are those who believe that death is not an end but a beginning, and there are those who do not believe this. We might borrow Augustine's metaphor and call these two classes, two "cities." The earthly city is made up of those who hope for nothing beyond this world. The city of God is made up of those who hope for an unimaginable and divinely bestowed fulfillment in eternal life beyond the grave.

Of course, since this is not the only factor discriminating among people, and since nobody in either group maintains unbroken consistency between this article of his belief and his daily existence, the members of the two cities easily mingle and do business with one another; make life and peace as well as war together. And no doubt there are ostensible Christians who are actually 100 percent citizens of that secular city, just as there are also "anonymous Christians" who belong to the other city even though they have never entered a church.

It is, though, preeminently characteristic of the authentic Christian to have a hope born of religious faith for immortality as an integral human person. That he must die he knows well enough, but he hopes to live again with flesh and spirit—with head and heart and hands, so to say. This hope can endure even though natural reason finds it incomprehensible, and despite the human tendency to shrink from dying. It is not really a hope for some self-enclosed kind of fulfillment. The Christian hope is for the gift of a transcendent union with God which no word or symbol can represent but in which alone the human person is completed. So Christians cherish their own image of death as a dawn and the coming of light, as an awakening to a life inconceivably more intense in an age beyond this *saeculum*. "You must wake up now. The night is almost over, it will be daylight soon . . ." (Romans, 13:11).

This division of judgment about the meaning of death is so radical a divergence that dialog between Christians and secular humanists might well start at this point. These humanists often say that the formulations of Christian faith are naïve, and perhaps they frequently are. To be a Christian is not automatically to be saga-cious and eloquent. But then it is fair for the Christian to ask the humanist for his answers to the problems of evil in general and death in particular. If the only response is that death is a full stop to the person's individual existence and that eventual betterment of human nature and social conditions will eliminate all but the unavoidable minimum of suffering (for some people will always smash up cars, fall off cliffs, have nervous breakdowns, or go blind), then we must say that this "answer" to those great questions is itself naïve and will not do. It might serve to effect a practical and stoical adjustment to the presence of death and evil, par-ticularly if these are not pressing too closely, but it will not heal the anguish that this century has learned to call "existential."

From its beginnings, though, Christianity has confidently made the overwhelming claim that Jesus, the Lord, has "abolished death, and he has proclaimed life and immortality through the Good News" (2 Timothy 1:10). The elements of that good news, as Catholic Christianity identifies them, can be gathered around three central themes: God, Christ, and the Church (the religious com-munity that calls Christ its Head).

It is not useful to represent being a Christian as location at a fixed point. It is rather like being somewhere along an inclined plane and more or less near its top. That summit would symbolize the ideal fullness of steadfast faith. But people can be dreadfully languid about believing and behaving like Christians. Still, they would not be accurately described as Catholics at all if they did not adhere, however weakly, to the essentials of this faith. The first of these essentials is surely acknowledgment of the existence of God as Creator of the universe and provident Father sustaining it—One Who has, therefore, an imprescriptable right to men's love and fidelity. This is the primary belief from which all else flows. As the young William James wrote to his friend Oliver Wendell Holmes in 1868: "If God is dead or at least irrelevant, ditto every-thing pertaining to the 'Beyond.' "[42] There would be no Christian answer to death apart from trusting faith in the God Who is described in the first and last books of the Bible as the beginning and the end of all things: " 'I am the Alpha and the Omega' says the Lord God, who is, who was, and who is to come, the Almighty" (Revelation 1:8). In the religious zone of life, as in any other, there is need for growth; in addition, given our inadequate concepts, it is always hard to speak of God. No doubt, in some Christians a reflective penetration of this first article of faith is barely em-bryonic, whereas in others it has indeed developed but the in-dividuals cannot voice it very well.

Still, most mature Christians will appreciate Newman's famous account, partial though it is: "Two and only two absolute and luminously self-evident beings, myself and my Creator."[43]

For these mature Christians the sense of a closeness to God begins with a sense of closeness to Jesus. This is not surprising, since Christians are by definition those who believe that Christ the Lord is authentically divine and authentically human, so that the Same Who is God is man. "To have seen me is to have seen the Father" (John 14:9). Words, again, which are the very definition of specifically Christian mysticism. For the heart of Christian faith is the conviction that God is met, known, and loved in Jesus as He could not otherwise have been. "No one can come to the Father except through me" (John 14:6). Saint Augustine summed it up in one of his memorable parallelisms: *Deus Christus patria est quo imus; homo Christus via est qua imus:* Christ-God the fatherland toward which we press; Christ-man the route whereby we go.[44]

Those who see in the Jesus Who died about A.D. 30 no more than a religious genius talk about the problem of continuity between this historical figure, a gifted Jewish teacher, and the Christ of faith saluted in the Creed. But for believers there is no real problem. They have no need to explain how there is a continuity, for they experience it. The Lord to Whom they pray is the Jesus Who was born in Galilee, baptized in the Jordan, and crucified on a hill outside the walls of Jerusalem. No doubt the conditions of His earthly existence and those of His resurrected state are very different, but He remains the One He is. Moreover, He is Himself a revelation about God, about the cosmos, and about the meaning of human life. About God whose inner life, according to Christian faith, is revealed to be that of a community of three eternal Persons, three centers of thought and love Who are distinct but coequal. About the universe, because the Son in taking flesh made clear the ontological goodness not only of human nature but of that entire creation of which man is part. Indeed, the universe itself in mysterious fashion has been, as Vatican II put it, emancipated by the Incarnation so that it may be fashioned anew and reach its fulfillment.[45] About man because Christ, without philosophizing at all, told men and women what they are and what they should become and made marvelously available the graces needed to attain this ideal.

In the moral order this ideal is a summons to make a radical transit from egoism to altruism. This requires that we be concerned for the welfare of all other human beings and that we show, or be ready to show them kindness. Reason declares this notion absurd, considering the multitudes of people, most of them naturally indifferent to or positively repelled by most of the others. The lives of saints, however, suggest that when a person has an intense conviction that Christ not only redeemed all men but actually knows, loves, and reaches out to them all, then he or she is able in some true sense to love every other human being in loving God in Christ. The first commandment is kept by keeping the second.

However, this Christian faith in Christ can be deficient both in understanding and in practice. Human intelligence has a hard time keeping the two affirmations about Him in adequate balance, and the perennial human tendency to extremes can easily lead to a depreciation of either the divinity or the humanity. In view of these historic errors, some contemporary theologians are saying that we badly need a development of Christology that will be loyal to the content of the dogma but will find fresh formulations, making it more intelligible and thereby diminishing misunderstandings and helping people assimilate it more effectively in their thought and action.

It can happen that a Christian will profess the fundamental faith in Christ and yet the Lord will seem hardly more to him than a distant historical personage. This second deficiency is more serious than the first, with which it is not necessarily connected. For there are simple people whose concepts are quite primitive but whose lives are steadily illuminated by a profound sense of union with Christ, whereas in others, presumably of greater formal religious literacy, this sense is unexpectedly absent. From those interviews with poor men and women, black and white, Robert Coles came away with the conviction, as he expressed it, that Jesus Christ lives on in their hearts and souls. One of them said to him: "We live on God; we wait on Him. After I've prayed to Him, I'll just think of Him, and sometimes I'll say to myself the words He said—that my mamma told to me back in Georgia."[46] This contrasts painfully with the remark of one Catholic nun: "I can no more speak to Jesus Christ than I can speak to George Washington."[47]

All this points to a central task of Christian education, which is to help people grow into the reality of a knowledge and intimacy with Christ. In The Fall, Camus had his antihero observe that there are those who love Christ, even among Christians, "but they are not numerous!" Perhaps the work of Christian education, precisely as such, is to make them more numerous.

But that religious dimension of life, like any other, develops gradually in a social climate and through interaction with others. The community particularly concerned with this growth is the Church, which has a complex social organization as its principal scriptural designations would suggest: It is called both the Body of

Christ and the People of God. But bodies are multicellular organisms, and a People is constituted from many subgroups, among which the family is primary and elemental. Thus Vatican II described the family not only as the first and vital cell of human society generally, but also as the fundamental unit in eccelesial society, as "so to speak, the domestic church."[48] Nowadays, Catholic families are organized, usually on a territorial basis, into parishes. The parishes of a given region constitute the diocese or local church, each with its own presiding bishop. The bishops, in turn, form a "college" in communion with the bishop of Rome, the pope, who by virtue of his office embodies the unity of all these churches both with Rome and with one another.

Children born into a Catholic family can, then, enter through that family into the wider religious community of the parish and the universal Church. If they do so, their religious development will be nourished by life in the Church just as other aspects of human growth are fostered in the family and all the various groups in civil society: the neighborhood, the town or city, the nation, the school, the job, and the voluntary organizations. Since man is essentially social, what Christians call redemption will be mediated in and through a society. For although there is indeed an individual religious experience, a person ordinarily is enabled to actualize it by having lived within the Church community. To share the life of this community is to find that the abyss between an invisible God and this visible world is bridged because, within the Church, God's presence is variously verified. He is encountered indirectly when His action is mirrored in the lives of good people. Above all, He is encountered in His Son when the Church communicates the Gospel word and when it makes Christ present in the liturgical cult. In this Eucharist, Catholics believe themselves to have an inexpressibly precious and real union with the living Lord. For believers, therefore, the Church serves as an efficacious sign or sacrament of Christ, not because of any natural social energies of its own but because it is made the instrument of divine action. Vatican II, indeed, saw the Church as a sign of two realities. It is a sign, in the first place, of God and of His presence in human history. It is also a sign of the unity that should exist among all men, a sign set above the nations to effect as well as to symbolize their longed-for unity.[49]

In practice, of course, obstacles often inhibit the realization of these ideals at each level. The council itself observed that believers can have more than a little to do with atheism among their fellowmen when their own failings conceal rather than reveal the face of God and religion.[50] Besides that, faith and practice in a Catholic community at a given time or place can be so indifferent that members of the Church itself hardly discern the divine face. Thus we find young people discovering the possibilities for an inner life by studying Hinduism, having left the Church without ever having heard of its own great mystical traditions. These failures, of course, are seldom deliberate. In times of extremely rapid social change, parents may be unable to introduce their children effectively into the Christian way of life. This is partly because the culture that shaped their own character and outlook was so different from that which shapes their children that the normal generation gap is unduly exacerbated. In many parts of the Western world in recent decades, men and women have found it easier to grow out of rather than into the religion of their parents. We hear often enough of prominent people, particularly in the arts and in the academic world, who were raised in Catholic families and schools but are now agnostics. This reminds us (if necessary) that the growth we have been discussing does not reach its term automatically. In the next two chapters we speak of certain aims of Christian education; before doing so, it would be sensible to acknowledge that these ideals, just because they are noble ones, are hard to realize to any considerable extent.

NOTES

1. The New Testament is, of course, in a class altogether by itself; it is the indispensable source for understanding what Christianity is about. But if I were asked to recommend a single book to be read along with the Gospels, it would be Luigi Santucci's *Meeting Jesus,* trans. Bernard Wall (New York: Herder and Herder, 1971). This is not, though, a summary of doctrine; perhaps the most useful of such summaries available is the well-known "Dutch Catechism" (with its supplement), which is not at all what the unalluring label of catechism suggests: *A New Catechism: Catholic Faith for Adults* (New York: Herder and Herder, 1972). There are three paperbacks that are still worthwhile, although they were written before the Second Vatican Council: Sebastian Bullough, *Roman Catholicism* (Baltimore: Penguin, 1963); Thomas Corbishley, *Roman Catholicism* (New York: Harper & Row; Harper Torchbooks, 1964) and N. G. M. Van Doornik, S. Jelsma, and A. Van de Lisdonk, *A Handbook of the Catholic Faith,* ed. John Greenwood (Garden City, N.Y.: Doubleday, 1956). Besides these epitomes, there are other statements, designed not so much to summarize Catholicism as to highlight and interpret some of its most significant aspects. Two distinguished older works of this genre are Karl Adam, *The Spirit of Catholicism,* trans. Dom Justin McCann, rev. ed. (New York: Macmillan,

1940) and Léonce de Grandmaison, S.J., *Personal Religion,* trans. Algar Thorold (London: Sheed and Ward, 1929). To them we might add Gaston Salet, S.J., *The Wonders of Our Faith,* trans. John Leonard, S.J. (Westminster: Newman Press, 1961); Hans Urs von Balthasar, *Who Is a Christian?,* trans. John Cumming (Westminster: Newman Press, 1967); and a little book by the distinguished Anglican theologian, E. L. Mascall, *The Christian Universe* (London: Darton, Longman & Todd, 1966).

2. See Alan Richardson, *An Introduction to the Theology of the New Testament* (New York: Harper & Row, 1958), pp. 24–25, 37. It is from this book that we borrow the translation of *zoe eonios* as "Life of the Age to Come." *Ibid.,* p. 71.

3. Henri de Lubac, S.J., "The Church in Crisis: Address at Saint Louis University, May 29, 1969," *Theology Digest,* 17 (Winter 1969), 325.

4. A wise English priest with years of experience as a pioneer in religious education remarked, by way of illustrating a point in the discussion of infallibility raised by Hans Kung's book *Infallible? An Inquiry:* " 'Faith' is another unserviceable word here. When Protestants, especially German Protestants, talk about 'Faith,' they include what Catholics normally mean by hope and charity; hence dialogue tends to become two deaf men arguing. My impression is that the endless dissertations and belly-achings about the nature and psychology of something called 'Faith', which ecumenically-minded Catholic theologians and catechists have been indulging in on the continent during the last twenty years, have been quite unrewarding and leading nowhere except into a land of perpetual mists." Canon F. H. Drinkwater in a letter to the editor, *The Tablet,* 225 (July 31, 1971), 747.

5. "Decree on Ecuminism" (*Unitatis Redintegratio*), November 21, 1964, in the English translation of *The Documents of Vatican II,* Walter M. Abbott, S.J., gen. ed. (New York: Guild-America-Association Presses, 1966), n. 14, pp. 357–358.

6. W. H. Lewis, ed., *Letters of C. S. Lewis* (London: Geoffrey Bles, 1966), p. 296. The line from Teilhard about the "new face of God" is taken from a letter he wrote September 4, 1951, which is quoted in Claude Cuénot, *Teilhard de Chardin: A Biographical Study,* trans. Vincent Colimore (Baltimore: Helicon, 1965), p. 319.

7. Henri de Lubac, S.J., *The Religion of Teilhard de Chardin,* trans. René Hague (New York: Desclee, 1967), p. 30.

8. This is from a statement made at the time of Pope John's death and quoted in a London Catholic paper, *The Universe,* June 7, 1963, p. 28.

9. See the essay by W. Norris Clarke, S.J., "Analytic Philosophy and Language About God," in George F. McLean, O.M.I., ed., *Christian Philosophy and Religious Renewal* (Washington, D.C.: Catholic University of America Press, 1966), pp. 39–73.

10. In this section on faith we rely heavily on the articles on this topic by Karl Rahner and Juan Alfaro in *Sacramentum Mundi,* Vol. II, pp. 310–325.

11. "Pastoral Constitution on the Church in the Modern World," *The Documents of Vatican II, op. cit.,* n. 59, p. 265.

12. See Saint Thomas Aquinas, *Summa Theologiae,* I, q. 54, a. 5, c. and *Scripta super libros Sententiarum,* Bk. III, d. 23, q. 1, a. 2. These and other citations, along with several paragraphs of the text here, are drawn from the author's essay, "The Scholastic: *Aquinas,*" in Paul Nash, Andreas M. Kazamias, and Henry J. Perkinson, eds., *The Educated Man: Studies in the History of Educational Thought* (New York: Wiley, 1965), pp. 126–127.

13. Paul VI, Homily delivered on June 29, 1971, in the Vatican Basilica and reported in *L'Osservatore Romano,* weekly English edition, July 8, 1971, p. 1.

14. "Dogmatic Constitution on the Church" (*Lumen Gentium*), November 21, 1964, *The Documents of Vatican II, op. cit.,* nn. 2, 13, 16; pp. 15, 30, 35.

15. "Pastoral Constitution on the Church in the Modern World," *Documents of Vatican II, op. cit.,* n. 22, pp. 221–222.

16. See J. P. de Caussade, S.J. (1675–1751), *Self-Abandonment to Divine Providence,* trans. Algar Thorold (Springfield, Ill.: Templegate, 1959), p. 5. This translation was first published in 1935. See also the abridgment of a lecture by Karl Rahner, "A Copernican Revolution: Secular Life and the Sacraments: I," *The Tablet,* 225 (March 6, 1971), 236–238.

17. "Pastoral Constitution on the Church in the Modern World," *The Documents of Vatican II, op. cit.,* n. 41, p. 240.

18. "There is something mystical associated with the word intuition, and any experience becomes mystical in the degree in which the sense, the feeling, of the unlimited envelope becomes intense—as it may do in experience of an object of art . . . For although there is a bounding horizon, it moves as we move. We are never wholly free from the sense of something that lies beyond." John Dewey, *Art as Experience* (New York: Putnam, 1934), p. 193. Of course, so vague an observation could be interpreted as implying nothing more than an aspect of strictly natural experience and as not pointing to anything beyond the limits of what moves in time and space. On the other hand, the theist may argue that Dewey was observing what he experienced and that, if this had been followed to its end, it would have led him to transcend the conditions of the physical universe.

19. Mary Crozier, *The Tablet,* 222 (April 20, 1968), 396.

20. See the article, "Faith," by Juan Alfaro in *Sacramentum Mundi,* Vol. II, p. 316.

21. On this point see Michael Simpson, S.J., "The Unbelief of Believers,"

The Month, 230 (July 1970), 6–10. Father Simpson discussed themes of an earlier essay by Johannes Baptist Metz, "Unbelief as a Theological Problem," *Concilium,* 6 (June 1965). One of its main points was put this way: "Both faith and freedom can develop in a person's life, and one may therefore speak of an element of unbelief or of lack of freedom which the person is always striving to overcome. This element of unbelief is not simply the result of a possible future action which may weaken one's faith, but is a central characteristic of our condition as finite believers. It is this basic unbelief which makes it possible for one to act in a way which contradicts one's faith. While this possibility always remains, it becomes less real the deeper that faith. No one however is a perfect believer, no one is fully free. The Christian life is a movement towards God, towards faith, towards freedom. It is against this underlying reality that difficulties with regard to particular expressions or practices of faith acquire their true perspective." *Ibid.,* p. 10.

22. This emphasis on the two themes of *teaching* and *way-of-life* is traditional, almost a formula. It serves in an essay by Claude Tremontant, who spoke of Christianity as a practice, or "way of life," and a theory, "Reflections of a Left-Wing Catholic," *Studies,* 54 (Winter 1965), 385.

23. Henry Thoreau, *Early Spring in Massachusetts* (Boston: Houghton Mifflin, 1881), p. 318.

24. Paul VI, address during the General Audience of July 7, 1971, *L'Osservatore Romano,* weekly English edition, July 15, 1971, p. 1.

25. Christian theologians and philosophers have often asked themselves whether the Bible and the faith of the Church mean to assert that some men have actually known of the existence of God and of the basic, natural ethical code by their own efforts alone or merely that this can be done, without saying whether it ever has been in fact. Perhaps in all such efforts there is also present a divine assistance that enlarges purely natural powers of intelligent insight. See Carroll Stuhlmueller, "The Natural Law Question the Bible Never Asked," *Cross Currents,* 19 (Winter 1968–1969), 55–67.

26. Henry Chadwick, *Early Christian Thought and the Classical Tradition: Studies in Justin, Clement, and Origen* (New York: Oxford University Press, 1966), p. 105.

27. Peter Matthiessen, *Sal Si Puedes: Cesar Chavez and the New American Revolution* (New York: Random House, 1969), pp. 195–196.

28. The vouchers for this remark of Dewey were reported in *The Dewey Newsletter,* a publication of the Co-operative Research on Dewey Publications at Southern Illinois University, 1 (July 1967), 12. Professor Edward J. Machle of the University of Colorado noted that he had heard Professor A. K. Reischauer say that Dewey had made this comment to him. Professor Culbert G. Rutenber, of Andover Newton Theo-

logical School noted having heard similar testimony from an American missionary to whom Dewey spoke.

29. E. L. Mascall, *The Christian Universe* (London: Darton, Longman and Todd, 1966), p. 17.

30. This kind of questioning is not confined to special Christian groups like the Hutterites living apart in small South Dakota colonies. It is done very sharply by a sophisticated sociologist, Philip Slater, in *The Pursuit of Loneliness: American Culture at the Breaking Point* (Boston: Beacon, 1970).

31. Geoffrey L. Heawood, *The Humanist-Christian Frontier* (London: S.P.C.K., 1967), p. vii.

32. Frederick Poorbaugh and Richard Stith, "Dilemmas in the Campus Ministry," *Yale Alumni Magazine,* 33 (June 1970), 28–29.

33. Robert Coles, "Talking with God," *Commonweal,* 91 (December 12, 1969), 332. See also a companion piece to this article in which Dr. Coles wrote of the religious experiences of these country people when they have moved to the cities: "The Lord of the Ghettos," *Commonweal,* 92 (November 13, 1970), 167–174. The full context of these materials is set out in the two volumes: Robert Coles, *Migrants, Sharecropper, Mountaineers,* and Coles, *The South Goes North* (Boston: Atlantic-Little, Brown, 1972).

34. James Collins, *The Emergence of Philosophy of Religion* (New Haven: Yale University Press, 1967), p. 480.

35. Alfred North Whitehead, *Process and Reality: An Essay in Cosmology* (New York: Macmillan, 1929), p. 517.

36. Alfred North Whitehead, *Adventures of Ideas* (New York: Macmillan, 1933), p. 41.

37. Rex Reed, "Signoret: I've Lived My Friend," *New York Times,* January 12, 1969, Section 2, p. 13.

38. W. H. Auden, *Cities Without Walls and Other Poems* (New York: Random House, 1969), p. 66.

39. Studs Terkel, *Division Street: America* (New York: Pantheon Books, 1967), p. 101. The remark of the Vietcong was quoted by Susan Sheehan, *Ten Vietnamese* (New York: Knopf, 1967), p. 166.

40. Rollo May, *Love and Will* (New York: Norton, 1969), p. 107.

41. Quoted by C. L. Sulzberger in his column "Foreign Affairs," in the *New York Times,* February 1, 1965, p. 22.

42. See Ralph Barton Perry, *The Thought and Character of William James,* briefer version (Cambridge: Harvard University Press, 1948), p. 97.

43. If these men and women grew up in Christian homes, they very likely believed in God before they ever heard of philosophical arguments for His existence. Yet it is a tenet of Catholicism that human intelligence is able to arrive with certainty at a natural knowledge of the existence of God the Creator from a knowledge of the world He has made. This

is worth noting in a book about educational ideals because it implies considerable esteem for the range and power of human thinking. Does it also imply that the existence of God can be proved in the technical sense which is attached to that term today? Some Catholic philosophers now prefer not to use the word *proof* because of its currently specialized and strictly formal usage. Their position has been lucidly expounded by W. Norris Clarke, S.J., "How the Philosopher Can Give Meaning to Language About God," in Edward H. Madden *et al.*, eds., *The Idea of God: Philosophical Perspectives* (Springfield, Ill.: Charles C Thomas, 1968), p. 1–27. Father Clarke wound up this paper by sketching a sophisticated form of the cosmological argument that concludes from the existence of the world-system as an interdependent whole to the need for a single, correlating intelligence, which is necessarily outside the system itself so that it can set the system up in the first place. An attractive, popular formulation of some other arguments was furnished by John C. Bennett, "In Defense of God," *Look,* 30 (April 19, 1966), 69–76. Dr. Bennett summarized four hints or intimations found in the world of human experience which are like signs pointing to the existence of God and are particularly effective if taken in conjunction with the Biblical revelation. These are: (1) the sense of an underlying meaning and organization in existence, (2) the sense we sometimes have of absolute obligation, (3) man's impulse to worship and serve something beyond himself, and (4) his actual experience of the operation of God's healing grace.

44. Saint Augustine, Sermon CXXIV, n. 3.
45. "Pastoral Constitution on the Church in the Modern World," *The Documents of Vatican II, op. cit.,* n. 2, p. 200.
46. Robert Coles, "The Lord of the Ghettos," *op. cit.,* p. 174.
47. Thomas E. Clarke, S.J., "Two Christian Styles," *America,* 124 (February 20, 1971), 177.
48. "Dogmatic Constitution on the Church," *The Documents of Vatican II, op. cit.,* n. 11, p. 29. See also the "Decree on the Apostolate of the Laity," *ibid.,* n. 11, pp. 502–503.
49. "Dogmatic Constitution on the Church," n. 9, and the "Decree on the Missionary Activity of the Church," n. 5, in *The Documents of Vatican II, op. cit.,* pp. 26 and 589, respectively.
50. "Pastoral Constitution on the Church in the Modern World," *The Documents of Vatican II, op. cit.,* n. 19, p. 217.

4

Toward a New and Transcendent Humanism: The Individual Goals of Education

Life . . . is always a synthesis.

Pius XII

Saint Thomas Aquinas advanced impersonally on his topics by way of searching and lucid analyses that neither required nor encouraged the coining of quotable maxims to make points. But on occasion he used a striking phrase to sum up; one of these concentrates is cited often and in a variety of contexts: "Man is inclined by his nature to know God and to live in society."[1]

We employ that epigram to mark off the grounds for dividing the materials of this and the following chapter. For Thomas's observation reminds us that every life has its private and individual as well as its public and social aspects. It has an inner side where that aspiration for the Absolute is found and an outer side centering on social participation. The aims of Christian education specify one or the other. These two segments are not separable, of course, but they are distinct. Catholicism insists on keeping that distinction in sight, resisting the reduction of the individual to his social functions alone and refusing to identify the total and ultimate vocation of the human person with the aims and welfare of earthly society. In fact, Catholicism asserts that communities exist for their members and not the other way round.

On the other hand, Catholicism knows that man is so essentially social that his capacity for a human life can only be actualized through living with others and that the more rational and truly humane society is, the better it will be for the individual's development of any and all of his potentialities, including the religious.[2]

Ideally, each of these two focal aspects should flourish and nourish the other. A man in whom the private segment of life had been consumed by public duties would be something of a slave, like a footman endlessly waiting in a despot's court, whereas a man who tried to dispense completely with human community would perish. A Robinson Crusoe, as Marx pointed out, survives in the wilderness only because he already dynamically possesses the forces of society within himself.

These two zones are, then, distinct and yet intrinsically related. Each needs to be developed both for its own sake and for the sake of the other, so that the person may be a healthy synthesis of individuality and sociality and so that he may have a significant inner and outer life. With this in mind, it seems reasonable to divide a summary of Catholicism's implications for education into two parts. These implications converge around three nuclear aims that can be recommended not just for Christians but for all men. Christianity, however, clarifies these basic educational concerns in its own way. The three objectives themselves are not to be thought of as placed side by side in separate compartments but as effectively synthesized to constitute one complete life, somewhat as matter and spirit constitute the human essence or the union of soil, air, and light constitutes the environment of life itself.

The first of these goals is that of a truly human education for every man and woman. The variables of time and place will color its content, but this substance should be animated by the basic aim of civilizing both intelligence and feeling and assisting the formation of conscience. This education must repudiate all distinctions of race, social class, and talent insofar as these support discriminatory practices in education. For a way must be found of providing everyone with the chance to examine life's central issues and to acquire the intellectual, cultural, and moral resources needed to meet these challenges. This is required because the Christian ideal of the educated person is not only universal in scope but humanistic in character. It can no more be satisfied with the pious boor than with the cultured unbeliever, because it envisions men and women who strive to be both truly human and truly Christian, knowing that unless they are both they cannot adequately be either. This is what Pius XII, who anticipated so many of the themes of Vatican II, had in mind when he wrote in his first encyclical: "There is no opposition between the laws that govern the life of faithful Christians and the postulates of a genuine humane humanitarianism, but rather unity and mutual support."[3] This is to say that genuine human growth provides the foundation for the two other goals we discuss: (1) the development of a true interior life whose most important element will be a prayerful familiarity with God, and (2) the development of the capacity for contributing to the welfare of others, particularly through one's work. The integral Christian must then be a combination of *Homo sapiens, Homo faber,* and *Homo viator*—man the mature thinker, man the worker, and man the traveler toward God.

In this chapter's account of the Christian specification of these three aims, we concentrate on those which can be thought of as actualizing the predominantly individual side of personality: humanistic culture for all and the nurture of the contemplative spirit. In the following chapter we are concerned with those purposes which are predominantly social, focusing on education for work and for building the kind of communities that Christians should intend in light of evangelical principles and the norms of healthy political philosophy. But it should be added that this ordering of materials is mostly a matter of convenience and emphasis, for when any one of these basic issues is occupying the foreground, the others furnish the background.

The intention throughout is to indicate how Catholic Christianity, within the framework of its distinctive affirmations, can provide intelligibility and unity for education. Although the Gospel has nothing to say about concrete school problems, there are characteristic decisions that ought to be made by people loyal to it when they respond to the four perennial categories of educational issues. These are the famous questions asking: Who should be taught? (which calls on one's understanding of what man himself is); What should be taught? Who should teach? and How?

Catholicism does imply some definite and distinctive judgments on these fundamental matters even if its contribution to the question of teaching methods is limited to a few highly general principles. A Christian is obliged, for instance, to honor every other person's innate dignity and to treat all others with consistent kindness. This, as we noted earlier, naturally rules out any cruel and coercive pedagogical procedures, as well as any that, however smoothly, exploit or manipulate students. It endorses those which promote an authentically human self-awareness and self-mastery. But for determining the precise techniques to be used, "science and experience," as Paul VI said, "can well suggest the best."[4]

The other three questions inquire about the character of individual fulfillment or about the nature of the communities that serve as favorable soil for the growth of this good man. How are such realities to be understood and achieved? How bring about the harmonious and interrelated unfolding, or "education," of the person's capacity for a self-realization that includes both friendship with God and an effective, fraternal sense of social responsibility? In outlining an answer these last two chapters are trying to indicate the chief features of what Paul VI, in his 1967 encyclical "On the Development of Peoples" *(Populorum Progressio)* called a new and transcendent humanism.

Just to propose such a scheme, however, raises the obstinate conviction that it needs justification. This is partly because much of what is said about educational objectives is so foggy or platitudinous, if not a toxic brew of half-truths, that alert readers may well feel they have had enough. Even precise and sober statements of genuine ideals can exasperate informed people who have a bleak perception of school realities and know how little the workaday world corresponds to the theorist's Kodacolor canvas. And of course this gap between principles and facts is more notorious and harder to accept when it characterizes Christian schools, as it always must to some extent. Yet if we never identified our aims, we would, as Aristotle knew, resemble men who had elected to be pilgrims or explorers rather than tourists, but still went journeying without any idea either of where they were going or where they wanted to go. And if we do discuss aims, would it not be better to state them as fully and ideally as possible and thereafter try to work out viable programs for realizing these ideals by degrees? In this way we might hope to bring about what Emmanuel Mounier, the French Catholic Personalist philosopher, called "the patient transformation of everyday life."

These reassurances are not likely to disarm every critic, especially since we maintain that the devising of those viable programs lies outside the scope of this book. When Charles Silberman in 1970 published *Crisis in the Classroom,* some reviewers complained that it was not enough to tell the public what was wrong with its schools. The author should also, they said, have spelled out detailed solutions. But that criticism was unfair and, in any case, does not seem applicable to our job here. For we are not cataloging the weaknesses of existing schools but inquiring about the general educational relevance of Catholicism; and Catholicism cannot be made to issue in a set of concrete school directives. Just as Christ was not an academic constructor of moral theory, Christianity is not a theory of education. But it does lay certain clear imperatives on educators, just as the Lord set moral ideals and duties before His followers.

"Still, you're fudging the question," someone may counter. "For actually education no more has aims outside the process itself than human growth does. This classic thesis of John Dewey is unassailable, and it won't do to fasten on education some potted objectives imported from Christianity."

But in fact we are not advocating the imposition of strictly extrinsic purposes on human development as a whole or on formal education in particular. We hope instead to identify those aims which are intrinsic to the evolution of a fully human person as Christianity understands this ideal. This presumes that there are such aims, but the presumption seems to be reasonable, as examples may show. A tree reaching maturity may have been cut for timber, and slaves may once have had their powers cultivated for the trade. But these cross marketing objectives of the entrepreneurs were not the intrinsic aims of growth and education themselves. On the other hand, such growth does have its goal because it is a movement toward ideal fullness. In the case of men and women, this plenitude, to describe it very generally, is that of a person capable of conceiving and effecting worthwhile purposes of his or her own.

Irving Babbitt, who was a critic of John Dewey in the 1930s, used to quote Aristotle's dictum that the first in importance is not the seed but the guiding ideal of the perfect flower. Yet Dewey could have agreed with this. For in *Democracy and Education,* he not only made that celebrated observation about education having no aims beyond itself, but he also formulated the aim of the ideal man: "It is not enough for a man to be good; he must be good for something. The something for which a man must be good is capacity to live as a social member so that what he gets from living with others balances with what he contributes."[5] Developmental processes in themselves may have only their own term as a goal; since, however, some kinds of growth are really destructive in light of the total picture (a cancer, for example, or the ripening of murderous skills in military recruits), the educator must know which ones are truly human and how to nurture these. In *Akenfield,* Ronald Blythe's memorable study of an English village, a young schoolmaster said: "I am interested, presumably, in showing people how to preserve the valuable part of themselves; only, as this profound thought has only just this minute occurred to me, I can't enlarge on it!"[6]

But if he did have time to consider and expand his comment, he would be found drawing on his understanding of human nature and destiny to answer questions such as: Which capacities of my students ought to be brought to perfect flower? From the whole range of possible human activities, to which ones should they be introduced so that this fulfillment may be attained? After all, some of the activities within school buildings are evil—shooting heroin in the washrooms—some are trivial, and some are valuable both in themselves and as means for achieving other values. If there is to be a really human growth, discriminations among available possibilities must be effected, and they will be made in light of one's whole theory of life. This is what Christians are doing when they theorize about education.

ON THE NOTION OF HUMANISM

With the needed help of divine grace, men who are truly new and artisans of a new humanity can be forthcoming. . . .

Vatican II
"The Church in the Modern World," n. 30.

In *Populorum Progressio,* that major statement quoted previously, Paul VI prefaced his reflections on the economic and social development of poorer nations with some remarks about every individual's right and duty of personal fulfillment. Several times he employed the term *humanism* for the view he was formulating, which, although hardly exceptional, was significant in its context. The context was that of a highly serious exposition by the chief spokesman for Roman Catholicism of certain demands made on himself and his fellow-Catholics by their faith:

In the design of God, every man is called upon to develop and fulfill himself, for every life is a vocation. . . . Endowed with intelligence and freedom, he is responsible for his fulfillment as he is for his salvation. . . . This harmonious enrichment of nature by personal and responsible effort is ordered to a further perfection. By reason of his union with Christ, the source of life, man attains to new fulfillment of himself, to a transcendent humanism which gives him his greatest possible perfection. This is the highest goal of personal development.[7]

Since *humanism* is a variable (not to say slippery) term, it may be useful to indicate the sense it has for Christians and the reasons for calling their outlook humanistic. We realize that *humanism* is sometimes understood as an alternative to religion. In that case, it means a rejection of religions in favor of exclusive concentration on humanity's strictly temporal welfare and on the promotion, without religious reference, of altruism in human relationships. This usage is common in England, where the British Humanist Society and the Humanist Teachers' Association are organized around these views. The Oxford English Dictionary's third definition of the word acknowledged this concept when it called *humanism* "any system of thought or action which is concerned with merely human interests (as distinguished from divine), or with those of the human race in general (as distinguished from individual)."

But there is no good reason for a single group or ideology to appropriate a useful noun from the common linguistic coffer, and it is perfectly possible to rework the foregoing definition so that by *humanism* we mean "any system of thought or action which is concerned with human interests both individual and collective." Now although Christianity is humanistic in this latter sense, it is of course much more than that. For instance, the full text of *Populorum Progressio* shows that Paul VI was advocating the same well-rounded development of the human powers that any responsible educator would propose; and the Second Vatican Council often made the identical point. But it is also true that pope and council believed that the summit of human development is that union with God for the fostering of which Christianity exists. Since the term *humanism* does not make this sufficiently clear, and since the term may also appear to have been compromised by having served to designate either antireligious forms of humanism or the narrow Renaissance tradition of polite classical learning, some Christians avoid or downgrade both the word and the idea. Thus Cardinal Suenens, in *The Nun in the World,* wrote: "What the world needs far more than Christian humanism is a thoroughly human Christianity."[8]

THREE HUMANISTIC STRANDS
IN BIBLICAL FAITH

Humanism, however, not only has a strong appeal to the sensibility of our times, but when it is applied to the Christian worldview, it brings into higher relief certain elements that ought not be neglected. For instance, three strands in the biblical faith of Catholicism powerfully foster a humanistic outlook: (1) the understanding of the universe as fundamentally good, (2) the emphasis on the intrinsic dignity or worth of each individual person, and (3) the instructive but hopeful reading of mankind's history. Taken together, they constitute a framework of meaning and optimism within which that concern for human interests can be sustained, and thus we might consider each of these themes in a bit of detail.[9]

In the first place, when Christians look at the natural world from whose materials we build our ambiguous civilizations, they find it fundamentally good, intelligible, and characterized by a certain order rather than by pure confusion. They appreciate what Einstein called "the grandeur of reason incarnate in existence." Nor are they surprised at the presence of this element, since they believe that the world comes from God and reflects His infinitely wise and benevolent purposes. It is God's imprint, *vestigium,* as theologians used to say—a created participation in the divine perfection. This is not to deny that in a dynamic, evolving universe, natural calamities will overtake men when they are caught up in the great movements of earth and stars, of winds, waters, and weathers. But surely everyone now recognizes that men are themselves the most dangerous element in the universe, all too often warring on their environment as well as on one another. For if man has indeed the nature and destiny that Christianity claims for him, then he must have the capacity for free choice; otherwise, he could not love. Yet if he is able to choose, he is also able to choose evil in pursuit of some presumptive good; and there is evidence enough that he frequently does so. But even though we now have the power to blow up a large part of our race along with the ground on which we stand, the earth itself remains basically favorable to human development. Without its air and produce, to take the most obvious cases, we should not live at all. If some philosophers assert contrarywise that the universe is radically evil and hence unfriendly, meaningless, and absurd, they must judge nihilism to be more logical than any humanism.

In this connection, it is worth noting that the two great humanistic systems competing with Christianity today—Marxism and the kind of non-Marxist secular humanism for which Dewey spoke— both discover some intelligible arrangement in the cosmos. This confirms the conviction that no humanistic footing can be maintained if the natural order is viewed as unrelieved chaos. Marx, indeed, through application of the dialectic to the data of nature and history, was sure that he had uncovered signs of an inevitable ascent toward a classless society that would fulfill every human aspiration. Dewey was less sanguine, since his Darwinian model was that of a more mysterious universe whose evolution could hardly be foretold. But he was optimistic because nature seems good and because man has the power to solve the problems he meets within his natural and social settings by the methods of pragmatic thinking that have been refined by science.

In the second place, Christianity regards mankind itself as the highest point of creation, even though, from one angle, it is also the most vulnerable. This is not to say that men are free to exploit the infrahuman world at will. In the great symbolic episode of Genesis, God says to Adam: "Fill the earth and conquer it." But a few verses later we read that Yahweh took "the man and settled him in the garden of Eden to cultivate and take care of it"—which is a way of saying that man is not to plunder or pervert nature. The New Testament provides the classic Christian metaphor of *stewardship* to express this obligation, indicating that a proper concern for ecology is a duty of religion as well as of common sense. Predictably enough, since the obverse side of a strength is often a weakness, man's capacity for willful destruction is the negative face of his greatest powers. For Christianity believes that every human individual has not only an animal dimension but is also a *person;* that is, a self-contained center of intelligence and freedom that, in fact, is destined never to be destroyed.

Prenatal genetic misfortunes or accidents during life may render a body incapable of sustaining the conditions needed for the exercise of thought and choice. But even in these sad cases, Christians affirm the presence of spiritual powers, although these powers cannot now be actualized. In short, every human being possesses this dignity, this intrinsic worth. No matter how ill-favored a man may be in other respects, no matter how poor in native endowments or external circumstances, he has these indestructible human excellences which his sins can betray but not annihilate. This conviction is nicely embodied in a bit of aphoristic dialogue from one of Western civilization's masterworks. In *The Magic Flute,* a priest of the vaguely Masonic realm in which the action unfolds is commenting to Sarastro, the presiding hierarch, about young Prince Tamino, who has stumbled into their sacred precincts: *"Bedenke: Er ist ein Prinz."* To which Sarastro replies truly enough, if somewhat sententiously: *"Mehr! Er ist ein Mensch!*

Mozart, like a number of Catholics on the continent in his day, was attracted by the Masonic ideals of human dignity and fraternity. But since these values are also honored in the Christian tradition, perhaps those eighteenth-century Catholics would not have looked for them in Freemasonry if they had been adequately expounded within the Church at that time.

That sense of brotherhood, for instance, is nourished not only by the great religious affirmations of the fatherhood of God and the universality of Christ's redemptive death but also by an appreciation of the fundamental dignity inhering in all men. This concept of the worth and richness of human personality is unfolded in Catholic thought by reflection on the four levels of synthesis that are embodied in every person.[10] For in addition to that combination of individuality and sociality already noted, each such person is an essential composition of flesh and spirit and also represents a synthesis of nature and grace (at least potentially) and of the specific human essence with a personal history. It will be useful to pause for a moment over this notion of man as a center constituted by these syntheses, for the idea provides a framework for what we have to say about aims of Christian education.

We know that men and women are such social beings that they

cannot mature and can scarcely survive apart from the societies within which they move. Every moment of our lives is enmeshed with the communities that sustain us—not just the intricate complex of contemporary social forms, but the whole great nerve of human history whose effects perdure even if its beginnings are lost to sight. This is obvious enough. Yet even though each one is truly a center of multiple relationships to others, each is still so individual that he possesses a personal existence that cannot be shared. People are able to communicate their possessions and even, more or less fully, their thoughts and feelings, but not their actual being. Kidneys can be transplanted, but not life or personhood.

This human person of whom we speak is clearly corporeal; but Christianity must affirm that he is more than a purely material organization, however complex, since otherwise he could not hope to transcend death. So far as philosophy goes Catholics can be Platonists or Aristotelians. They may think of man as a soul needing a body or as a natural composite of soul and body. Some maintain that spirit is qualitatively different from matter; others may say that the difference is only one of degree. But in any case, all agree that human persons are necessarily compositions of body and consciousness—spirit in the world, to use the epigrammatic title of a book by Karl Rahner. Saint Thomas Aquinas made the same point when he observed that man is unique because he is composed of a bodily and a spiritual substance and is, therefore, set between two worlds with his soul situated on the boundary between heaven and earth.[11]

Christian philosophers and theologians have also customarily agreed that man is most characteristically himself in his thought and his freedom of choice. But not everyone concurs. There are thinkers who insist that man's sexuality is more significant than his intellectuality. There are others who believe that accenting intelligence means snobbishly dissociating man from the animal part of his own nature and from his kinship with the beast. Yet to say that man is most himself when he is most rational and free is not to disparage his physicochemical, instinctual, and sense activities; nor is it to deny that people often act in accordance with sensory attractions or emotional tides rather than reason's judgments. Man is certainly more than intelligence. The uniqueness of the human condition, however, cannot be located in those qualities of extension, sensation, and sexuality which he shares with the lower animals, although these are all parts of his nature and are either necessary or influential for thought. Folk wisdom recognizes the hierarchy here when it calls the eyes the windows of the soul and the brow the seat of intelligence. In September 1959, Nikita S. Khrushchev gave memorable expression to this kind of perception. His California tour had included a visit to the 20th Century-Fox sound-stages, where a scene from *Can-Can* was being filmed with "sixteen screaming chorus girls who spent more time bottoms up than on their feet." Emerging from the studio, the disenchanted Khrushchev observed with that earthy eloquence of which he was master: "Humanity's face is more beautiful than its backside."[12]

Of course giving primacy to intelligence and will does not logically require depreciating any other aspect of human nature. On the contrary, Christianity teaches that sexuality and feeling are themselves enhanced and enriched when they are drawn into the zones of thought and freedom. For then they can become vehicles for expressing and sustaining a distinctively human love between husband and wife or for awakening and feeding the impulses of art. Besides, thought itself is often interwoven with affectivity which, as Père Rousselot pointed out years ago, can itself heighten perception.[13] Thus the optimist is stirred by all things and draws from each its smiling aspect, and the pessimist says with Jaques in *As You Like It:* "I can suck melancholy out of a song as a weasel sucks eggs."

But here we are underlining the preeminence of rationality and liberty because it is intelligence that enables men to become self-conscious and transcendent, whereas freedom makes possible not only friendship among human persons but even friendship with God. Self-consciousness and transcendence are only current terms for qualities appreciated long before now. In the *Summa contra Gentiles,* for instance, Aquinas ran through a contrast of plant, animal, and intellectual activity and concluded that the highest grade of life is the intellectual, since it manifests the greatest degree of knowledge and self-movement.[14] For man can be aware of himself. He can reflect on his actions and, in the very act of knowing an object, also know himself, the conscious subject, and know that he knows. As we would put it today, man is able to say "I," since he can predicate his activity of himself. That is part of what it means to be a person, and it points to a spiritual constituent in personality, since sheer matter has not this capacity for bending wholly back on itself in a complete reflection, just as no knife can cut itself.

Yet although Thomas saw man as a being-in-the-world whose highest distinction is that he thinks, that was not all he had to say. His interest as a metaphysician was not so much in essences as in existence itself, and existence is necessarily a source of activity.

Thus Aquinas paid considerable attention to human action, and in doing so he concluded that the supreme activity of the good man is charity, which is the highest form of love—love of God and love of all other human persons as an expression of that love of God. This in turn builds human communities because it creates among men that fraternal spirit which is the best social cement. Love effects the union of hearts that supports the tranquillity and order in which peace consists; love is the real condition of justice in all societies from the family to the State. Christian humanism, we might say, aims at developing rationality as the environment for a life of authentic love.

Such a life would be scarcely possible if men could only respond as animals do to the stimulation of physical forces within and outside themselves. But intelligence is also the power that releases men from total dependence on these material conditions and allows them to transcend their situation to some extent. In the north woods, as winter approaches, the birds go south and bears crawl into caves. But the people of Minnesota continue about their business even when the thermometer falls well below zero. The practical function of intelligence makes it possible for them to overpass both a hostile environment and the grooves of sheerly instinctive conformity to its conditions. Of course, this transcendence has limits, for men are firmly rooted in this world, being neither divorced from its context nor strangers to it. At the same time, since intelligence is so effective a tool for controlling and transforming the earthly setting, we are to some degree independent of the natural elements.

In the opinion of religious men, this transcendence is most nobly realized when the human person arrives at an awareness of the reality of the unseen God and reaches Him in that charity of which we spoke. Although the mind cannot reach God immediately, the heart can, because love, as Aquinas noted more than once, always unites the lover directly to the beloved. But this ascent, according to Catholicism, is only accomplished because God enhances the natural powers of intelligence and will with those enabling gifts called grace. These gifts, though, are offered to everyone; thus each individual is actually or potentially that third synthesis—of nature and grace. Christian education, as we say in some detail presently, has as one of its chief aims the fostering of that divine union by helping people become more aware of its importance.

Finally we should note that Christians appreciate, as most people do, that each of us is a being with a history of his own. Not only do we share the specifically human essence with our ancestors and with one another, but each of us has realized it amid events and personal relationships that form the stuff of his individual story. Not only are we shaped by living in this epoch rather than that, but we have been irrevocably fashioned by our own local events. Mozart had his distinctive experiences, and so has that Bronx dentist, and so have we all. To be human is to be historical—not simply because one lives at this time rather than that or in this community and not elsewhere, but because there is a sequence and a meaning to the happenings of one's life, however obscure this may be.

Catholic education, just as any other, must take into account the influence of social and historical settings because their impact is quite ineradicable. In the course of this accounting, Catholicism acknowledges a profound effect that touches all men but had its origins at the very beginning of the human story long before history was recorded at all. The doctrine of Original Sin, which expresses this belief, is exceedingly mysterious because some aspects of it are scarcely yet clarified. But one element of the dogma that has special interest here is its insistence on the solidarity of the human race both in a nature and in beginnings common to all. Biblical faith teaches that each person was somehow involved in certain historic events of crucial significance. Saint Paul, for instance, arrived at the conclusion of the existence of a first sin and its universal effect by reflecting on the Christian belief that Christ died for all men so that, through faith in Him, all might share in His resurrection. But if all need redemption, all must at the outset of their lives be in a condition that can by analogy be called sinful.

Personal sin is a moral disorder that alienates a man from God because it embodies a willfull preference for man's own purposes, even at the expense of those divinely intended. When Christians realized that all men required the benefits of Christ's redemptive death in order to enter on friendship with God, they concomitantly realized that this must mean that all are born without that gift. Since, however, this unhappy estrangement is not what God originally proposed, it amounts to moral disorder. But how that alienation came about and how its willfulness involves even those born today remains obscure. Still, this much would be said by those who accept the doctrine: At the beginning of the human story, so inconceivably long ago, the first generation of men must have broken their loving relationship to God by a seriously disproportionate self-reference. The suggestion that this sin was some injury to human brotherhood is both appealing and logical because nearly every sin damages the love we owe to others.[15] This generation, being the first of our species, gave a direction to human history that affects all who were virtually present in our solidarity with those first human beings.

But Catholics also believe that in anticipation of Christ's life and death, His grace was available from the moment of that first sin, so that men were never actually without the means for reestablishing friendship with God. This friendship, however, is not now communicated to us simply because of our membership in the human race. We acquire it by our own encounter with the Lord. This may be accomplished for children through an experience that begins when they are inserted through Baptism into the Christian community. It may, as we noted in the preceding chapter, occur for adults when the turnings of their personal histories bring them to the question: What think you of Christ?

Agnostics are ready enough to accept such personal histories as factual phenomena; but the reading of universal history proposed by the doctrine of Original Sin is another matter. The distaste this arouses is intensified when it is mistakenly interpreted to mean that human nature today is essentially evil. But in fact Catholicism insists both on the ontological goodness of this nature and on the primary importance of moral freedom. Man, as one theologian put it some years ago, "considered simply as natural man, is as whole today, in intellect and will, as was man regarded in his purely natural endowment when he came from the creative hand of God."[16] For what primordial sin is understood to have lost was that original bond of divine friendship and the gifts that went with it. This friendship can only be regained by a man's free acceptance of it, and therefore freedom is extolled in some of the most moving Gospel passages: "You will learn the truth and the truth will make you free. . . . If the Son makes you free, you will be free indeed" (John 8:32, 36). It is not surprising, therefore, that Vatican II frequently adverted to the conditions required for the growth of this freedom and complained that it "is often crippled when a man falls into extreme poverty."[17]

The teaching about Original Sin, then, does not say that man has a depraved nature; rather, it reminds him that he does have a seriously divided one. Most of us discover the evidence for this within ourselves. We know that to be human is to be capable of wrongdoing because it is to be free to choose pseudovalues over authentic ones or to omit good deeds out of cowardice or sloth. We can readily appreciate the famous words of Paul: "I cannot understand my own behavior. I fail to carry out the things I want to do, and I find myself doing the very things I hate" (Romans 7:15). Yet Paul was not insuperably cast down; for if he believed in the reality of original as well as personal sin, he also believed that Christ had overcome the first and that His help was at hand to vanquish the second.

Since every Catholic Christian has the same belief, his radical outlook should be one of qualified optimism. This attitude is a logical result of his accepting those three features of biblical faith summarized here, and it is a hallmark of Christian humanism. No doubt the world of our civilizations is the arena of that fierce conflict between light and darkness to which the Fourth Gospel firmly points. Nevertheless, Christians believe that the conflict is not between absolute good and absolute evil, and its outcome is not in doubt. The ultimate victory for humanity has already been secured in the Easter resurrection of the Lord. It remains for each individual personally to appropriate the fruits of this victory by steadily trying to embody the two great commandments in his own life. But the grace of Christ works unceasingly to help each one accomplish this universal human vocation, and if no men are wholly virtuous, neither are any irredeemably bad.

Christians can, therefore, accept the fact of the hostile divisions created by basic human egoisms without being overwhelmed by their very existence. Their faith tells them how ancient these roots are and promises that they will be overcome when the fullness of the kingdom arrives. That kingdom will come in God's own time; meanwhile Christians can work enthusiastically alongside all men of good will for the amelioration of social and individual evils, without supposing that their efforts will banish these completely. Christians are obliged to struggle for the conversion of deserts into fertile ground because their humanity requires them to do the work of men. But they can settle for morally acceptable compromises and balances of power and put up with temporal disappointments and aridities all the better for believing in eternity. If they thought that man himself and his life in this world were the only and self-sufficient purposes, they should become just as pessimistic as most thoughtful secularists are today. But since their humanism is open to the reality of God and is therefore transcendent, Christians do not make mankind its own final goal and they do not believe that human persons are confined to time and space. On the contrary, they are destined for an Age-to-Come. Paul VI, often pictured in the press as rather somber, said quite serenely in his Easter message of 1965: "Optimism will prevail." No doubt this is a matter more of faith than of vision; but if we are able to entertain this kind of moderate Christian optimism, it will serve as bracing tonic for the humanistic conviction.

WHO SHOULD EDUCATE?

Now, for the first time in human history, all people are convinced that the benefits of culture ought to be and actually can be extended to everyone.

Vatican II,
"The Church in the Modern World," n. 9.

The notion of Christian humanism expressed above is still indistinct, but it can be sharpened by identifying some of its specific characteristics. It might be helpful, though, to preface this discussion with a general answer to that general question: Who should teach? The trouble is that "teaching" is an ambiguous term. In itself the concept is not confined to schooling, and yet the word is apt to awaken fantasies of school and the whole apparatus of formal education. A few additions to the notion of education sketched out in the second chapter may provide some useful clarifications. It was said there that the process of education is fundamentally the process of passing on a people's way of life. We tried to fend off the outrage of radical theorists by insisting that to say this is not the same as saying that education is a defense of the status quo. For in order to reject its evil elements and purify the others, all education should include a critical examination of the culture from which it issues.

Who are the chief agents of this educational process? Any answer, whether Christian or other, should acknowledge three principles. The first is implied in a distinction that has probably been known for ages and was emphasized by Saint Thomas Aquinas as long ago as the thirteenth century. When he analyzed the act of teaching he differentiated between *inventio* (or discovery, learning-by-one's own efforts) and *disciplina* (or learning-through-being-taught-by-another).[18] Following on this distinction, Thomas made two wise observations. He remarked that discovery or independent investigation is the better of these two ways because it indicates greater power in the learner and involves him in direct contact with realities without a teacher's mediation. Think of gifted children who, in effect, teach themselves to read. We know from our own experience that what we have learned by ourselves is usually more vivid and meaningful than what we have been taught. Thus we understand the assertion that much the best education a man gets is the one he gives himself. But most of us lack the time or the talent to learn all we need to know without some teacher's help. The chief value of learning-through-teaching is economic. Few people would have the leisure, the courage, or the energy, even if they had the resources, to learn without any assistance from others.

When others help us learn, however, they would do well to recall Aquinas' second observation. Since the way of personal discovery is primary and better, he said, teachers should model their method on the one naturally used by a man when he is learning through discovery. This is an application of Thomas's more general insight that whenever an effect can be produced either by nature or by art, the method of art should be as much as possible like that of nature. Thus he observed that a physician heals a man with an infection by giving him medication that reinforces the body's own curative powers. The analogy is good even if the medical science is inaccurate. The effective teacher contrives for his pupils an experience as much like that of independent discovery as is feasible. Without becoming further entangled in teaching theory, then, let us simply say that the first reply to "who should educate?" is, in the truest sense, "the learner himself," for he is the chief agent of his own learning.

The second principle to be underlined is embodied in the recognition of parental rights in education by American law. Catholicism would simply add that this right is primary and rooted in human nature; it is acknowledged, not bestowed by the state. Thus Vatican II in its "Declaration on Christian Education" noted that parents are "the first and foremost educators of their children. Their role as educators is so decisive that scarcely anything can compensate for their failure in it."[19] This parental right is first not only in time but in importance. The point needs emphasizing because throughout history many political leaders as well as some churchmen have been inclined to bully the family and usurp its functions. The state has been the worst offender because it has the physical force needed to implement its decrees, whether these be the despotic ones of a Stalin or the small-minded ones of county officials in Iowa carting Amish children away to public schools. But Church leaders may also overreach themselves by abusing their moral authority. The danger of doing this is diminished, however, if care is taken for exact analysis of the religious society's own right to teach.

On the last day of 1929, Pius XI issued an encyclical on "Christian Education of Youth." It was written in the heyday of Italian Fascism, with its propensity for marching little boys off for early Sunday morning military drill. It is not surprising, therefore, that this document insisted strongly on the Church's right to educate, which it described as "preeminent." But that term in itself merely means "more noble, superior in excellence." It does not mean that the Church is the primary educator or that it has universal jurisdiction over all the other agencies of education. No doubt, a bishop can and should warn his fellow-Catholics of the risk their children would incur if they were sent to a school that would certainly corrupt them; however, the parents would be expected to know as much themselves. If they do not, this suggests that the church in their part of the world is failing in its own specific educational tasks. In any event, the case is rather hypothetical in free countries, and in totalitarian states neither family nor Church can resist civil power successfully. But granted that the Church must teach the Gospel message and protest against social evils in schools as well as elsewhere in society, this does not mean that its own right to educate is universal in extent. What right, for instance, has either Church or state to manage the toilet-training of young children? None. Of course, if parents physically abuse their children the Church may admonish and the state prosecute them. But this does not mean that either agency has an all-encompassing power that virtually includes the family's prerogatives.

Those prerogatives do not imply, of course, any right to withhold education, but rather to give and oversee it. The American legal tradition testifying to this was enunciated twice in the 1920s by the United States Supreme Court. In *Meyer* v. *Nebraska* in 1923 the Court observed that "it is the natural duty of the parent to give his children education suitable to their station in life."[20] Two years later, in the celebrated "Oregon" case, *Pierce* v. *Society of Sisters, Pierce* v. *Hill Military Academy,* the Court, in a sentence quoted by Pius XI in his aforementioned encyclical, said: "The child is not the mere creature of the state; those who nurture him and direct his destiny have the right, coupled with the high duty, to recognize and prepare him for additional obligations."[21]

Why should the Court have spoken this way? Is it not because education in a true sense is the continuation and completion of procreation? What parents intend is to rear other men and women. The new-born infant is only potentially a person in the full psychological sense of the term. The point can be clarified if we think of the case of a brief, illicit liaison that ends before the child casually begotten from it is born. Suppose that this child is adopted by a couple who bring him up with loving care, school him, and guide him to adulthood. Who is more properly called the father of that child—the man who was all to him that a father could be save for the fact of generation or the man who was his father only in the biological sense? To fulfill the vocation of parenthood necessarily means to educate, and to deny it would be in a very real sense to destroy the role of parent.

American practice has honored these parental rights by keeping some measure of control over public education as close as possible to the local communities. In other words, our constitutional tradition recognizes implicitly that when political society enters the field of education, it finds the family already there. Many American Catholic educators have further concluded that if the state is fully to acknowledge this natural primacy, it ought to envision its own educational function as, in the first place, that of helping families.

In any case, the principle of parental rights has certain current practical corollaries. For instance, it ratifies the basic aim of those decentralization plans which propose to make more effective the families' involvement in the control of education in the big cities. It also provides an argument for public aid to nonpublic schools. For if parents have the first right to educate, the state might well help them exercise it by helping them select their children's school, so long as this school prepares literate and competent citizens, which society must have. No doubt the nation's effort to achieve a racially integrated society could be impeded if nonpublic schools were segregated enclaves. But racial discrimination is forbidden to Christian schools by an imperative far more sweeping than the 1954 decision in *Brown* v. *Board of Education of Topeka.* For the Catholic Church, as the Second Vatican Council said, "rejects as foreign to the mind of Christ, any discrimination against men or harassment of them because of their race, color, condition of life, or religion."[22]

And it ought to be possible to have Christian schools capable of responding to this imperative. This leads to the third principle to be acknowledged in answering the question, Who should educate? Just as Catholics recognize the nation's stake in education and its correlative right to educate, so they claim for their religious community its own right to educate and to conduct schools. A century and a half ago, in fact, many Americans would have contested the assertion that the state has a right to maintain schools, insisting that education belongs to the family and to the Church. Nowadays, it is clear that the tens of millions of young people cannot be introduced to our complicated civilization which, like a Russian Easter egg, encloses concentric cultures, subcultures and subsubcultures, unless the agencies of the civil community carry a large share of the work. In these circumstances we perceive more easily than our ancestors did both the importance of the larger social aims of education and the obligation of the nation to see that these objectives are reasonably well attained. Civil society has, therefore, a right to educate which includes the maintaining of its own schools and other educational agencies. It is also entitled to make sure that nonpublic schools meet minimum health and safety standards and are academically respectable. Vatican II's "Declaration on Christian Education" acknowledged these rights and duties of the political community clearly enough. But since the history of the past two centuries suggests that states have a tendency to monopolize schooling and to expand their overseership, the same decree rather anxiously warns against such tendencies.

No doubt the council's decree reflects the bishops' interest in underscoring the importance of the right to conduct church schools. The Catholic community sees itself as commissioned by its Lord to preach His message to every generation and in all parts of the world. That is to say, it must teach. This has to be done continually, since the community must recruit its membership afresh with each new generation. One of its principal and hardest tasks is to show young people how to synthesize the Gospel and the secular culture in their own lives so as to be both fully human and fully Christian. A school that effectively educates in the arts and sciences and at the same time contributes to religious growth would seem to be the best environment and instrument for realizing this synthesis. We turn now to spelling out some of the materials of this synthesis; but as we do, let us keep in mind what has just been said about the variety of educational agencies, and let us not suppose that every aim of Christian education has to be sought through formal schooling. Since the forces of education are several, the humanization of man is really accomplished by all these forces working in concert.

HUMANISTIC EDUCATION FOR ALL

The question of who should be educated is so closely joined to other considerations that if we tug at it even lightly we dislodge whole philosophies of human nature and society, along with some central theological themes. Of course, the question is simply redundant when posed abstractly, since everyone in every society must get some education if that society is to survive. Moreover, the aim of universal literacy is uncontested today. It would be useless, therefore, to ask this question without a certain amount of particularization. What we really want to ask is this: Supposing that there is an ideal of humanistic culture, for whom should education make it available? Christians must reply: For all men and women without any discrimination, even if differences in ability require variations of pace and depth in the pursuit of this goal. This humanistic culture is not the whole of the education of Christians, but it is an important part.

That generic description of education as the passing on of a people's way of life does not itself rule out elitist or class-conscious or discriminatory educational schemes. But the Christian doctrines of the solidarity of all men in a common nature and destiny and of the dignity of personhood in each individual do require that each one be educated to bring to the highest feasible fulfillment his powers of intelligence and will. It will be generally agreed that purely human culture includes arts and sciences that are the finest instrumentalities for this growth.[23] They must be accessible to all just as the means for sound physical development must be. In short, Christians should adapt Dewey's famous recipe for elementary schooling and make it their objective for the total educational experience of all persons: "What the best and wisest parent wants for his own child, that must the community want for all of its children."[24] And in fact, the Second Vatican Council spoke this way more than once:

Now, for the first time in human history, all people are convinced that the benefits of culture ought to be and actually can be extended to everyone. . . . Energetic efforts must also be expended to make everyone conscious of his right to culture and of the duty he has to develop himself culturally and to assist others. For existing conditions of life and work sometimes thwart the cultural strivings of men and destroy in them the desire for self-improvement. This is especially true of country people and laborers.[25]

The title of this chapter has been drawn from Paul VI's appeal for a humanism that would be both transcendent and new. Its trancendence consists in liberation from the conditions of sheer matter by the cultivation of intelligence and particularly by opening the human spirit to an awareness of God. The newness lies in the attempt to make this ideal available for everyone. Such a humanism has by no means been achieved either in the United States or anywhere else; yet it has attracted generous spirits for several centuries. That true Christian, the Moravian bishop John Amos Comenius (1592–1670), envisioned it in his plan of *pansophia*—universal knowledge for all men. At about the same time, Saint John Baptist de la Salle (1651–1719) was establishing the Brothers of the Christian Schools to teach young people we would call "underprivileged." The Brothers did their work so well that in 1763 an outraged French politician, Louis Réné de Ja Chalotais, complained in an "Essay on National Education" that people who had no need of such skills were learning to read and write and would no longer be satisfied to follow out their dull daily round. This dissemination of cultural resources, proposed by Marx as the goal of a perfect Communist state, has not been realized, even though the workers in Hungarian factories used to be marched down the street to compulsory attendance at approved art exhibits.

However, a variety of ideological, ethnic, or economic prejudices have always been at hand to explain why this ideal is bad, stupid, or simply impossible. Both Plato and Aristotle, for all their unequaled genius, displayed the typical bias of the free, well-to-do Greek intellectual toward ordinary work and the ordinary people who do it. In the *Republic* Plato left the artisan class out of his plans for schooling. These craftsmen presumably had to learn their trades, but they were not eligible for the publicly furnished education in music, poetry, and mathematics, which the soldiering class receives, and much less do they share the studies of the ruling elite in higher mathematics and metaphysics. Aristotle in the *Politics* said flatly that the best form of state will not allow mechanics to be citizens because men leading mechanics' lives cannot pursue the excellences of philosophical contemplation as good citizens must.

Other forms of educational discrimination have arisen from economic conditions. Marx pointed out in *Capital* that the factories of his day prospered most when the minds of the workers were least consulted and the workers were treated as parts of a machine. Indeed, some eighteenth-century manufacturers, he said, preferred to employ the mentally retarded for operations that were trade secrets. We hear an echo of this sentiment in the comment of the North Carolina sawmill owner who in 1900 specified "the uneducated negro to be the best we have for drudgery."[26]

Then there is that oldest form of prejudice in education, which has been a particular expression of a more general discrimination against women. As long as women were barred from anything more than elementary schooling, it was that much easier to keep them from participating in business, politics, or the arts.

But not every discriminatory school plan is prompted by the kind of vulgar prejudice that answers the question "Who should be educated?" by saying: not workers, not women, not blacks. Sometimes the discrimination is the product of a bias favoring an aristocracy not of birth or wealth but of talent. Thomas Jefferson, nowadays revered as the titular philosopher of the American democratic idea, proposed a meritocracy for his Virginia. He would have divided the state into districts five or six miles square and set up an elementary school in each. Every year a school visitor from each of these institutions would "chuse the boy of best genius" from among those whose parents could not pay for more schooling. This boy would be sent on to one of twenty grammar schools to study Latin, Greek, geography, and higher arithmetic. The favored boys would spend a year or two at grammar school, whereupon the best of them would be kept for a full six years "and the residue dismissed." By this means, said Jefferson, coolly, "twenty of the best geniuses will be raked from the rubbish annually, and be instructed at the public expense, so far as the grammar schools go."[27]

Still it may be said by perfectly generous people that the notion of a professedly intellectual and humanistic education for all men and women is exceedingly difficult, if not impossible, to realize and, therefore, to propose it is fanciful. And yet . . . there are these considerations. On the one hand, there is the conviction in the Atlantic community of nations ever since Periclean Athens that the fulfillment of free men lies in their development of intelligence and character and their sharing in all the fruits of civilization. These are the values Aristotle called "the goods of the soul." On the other hand, we have the Christian insistence that the criteria that would bar certain people from access to these goods are all irrelevant. For within the Church itself there must be no discrimination: "You are, all of you, sons of God through faith in Christ Jesus . . . and there are no more distinctions between Jew and Greek, slave and free, male and female, but all of you are one in Christ Jesus" (Galatians 3:26–28). The logical conclusion for Christian education, even in the matter of teaching secular arts and sciences in schools, is that cultivation of intelligence and the appropriation of human culture must be the aims intended for everyone.

This means that Christians cannot accept for themselves nor approve for public education any theory of aims that proposes two essentially different kinds of general education—one for the gifted and one for the less gifted. By general education we mean substantially what the 1945 Harvard Committee meant when it defined the term as that part of a man's whole education which looks first of all to his life as a responsible human being and citizen as distinguished from his education for a particular kind of work.[28] It is not necessary to maintain that this basic humanizing education can only be provided in schools or that it requires continual school attendance for everybody from the ages of five to twenty-one or more. The family will certainly be involved here, and the Church should be. A variety of other agencies could be called on, and the program might be spread across the whole of a long life in ways not yet dared. Common schooling ought not to contradict this ideal, and yet it usually does in practice. Many European nations regularly distribute children into two streams after elementary education; one group is headed for the university by way of an academic program, and the other after some further general or technical training for lower-level jobs. The American system, to be sure, does not explicitly ratify this kind of division, but it is no less real here. A boy who goes to grade school in Scarsdale or Grosse Pointe and then to St. Paul's has an education, both at home and in school, which differs in kind from that experienced by boys who go from ghetto elementary schools to the vocational programs of urban high schools enrolling thousands.

We have no scheme to replace this widely recognized condition; stating it, however, serves to note its incompatibility with the purest Christian as well as democratic ideals. To introduce a better practice everywhere may seem impossible, since it would require radically changing the civilization of a nation whose population exceeds 200 million. But even small measures toward that end will be neglected if we do not subscribe to the ideal of full humanistic development for each citizen and incline instead to see them all as so many individuals ordered to an overarching social purpose. Two contrasting proposals for American secondary education will illustrate the differences in approach that are possible here.

In 1960 James B. Conant proposed that American high schools recruit academically talented youth of both sexes for the professions and mobilize the rest through a strong vocational program for highly skilled work in modern industry.[29] It should be added that Conant supposed that the youth in vocational training would also spend half their time on English, social studies, science, and mathematics. He might also have noted, although he did not, that a vocational education can itself be genuinely humanizing and can serve to mature imagination, intelligence, and character. Finally, it should be pointed out that Dr. Conant made these proposals to meet what he considered to be national needs in an hour of crucial technological competition with the Communist bloc. If the existence of a free nation required this educational design, no doubt it could be defended. But apart from extreme crises, Christians will find more attractive another proposal made the same year by a Catholic priest-educator of vast experience. In an essay entitled "Excellence for Whom?"[30] Lorenzo K. Reed, S.J., advocated a new kind of comprehensive high school for Catholic students which would give every boy or girl an academic education up to the very limit of his or her capacities. The program would, of course, be so constructed that students of varying abilities moved at different speeds and tackled the materials at different levels. But the humanizing contact with languages and literature, mathematics and science, history and theology, art and music was not, on this reckoning, barred to the future artisans (Plato's men and women of bronze), nor doled out to them in limited portions. For if there is a basic educational experience that cultivates the universally human and brings the intellectual and moral resources up to their highest power, then this is the best foundation for the vocations of housewife, scientist, corporation manager, physician, mechanic, artist, lawyer, or monk. And if there is no such basic educational experience, why do the rich and talented get precisely this kind of liberal schooling while the poor do not?

At any rate, since Christians believe that every man and woman is a person by reason of possessing those capacities for thought and freedom, they must logically defend for each of these persons an education providing maximum cultivation of these powers. This is not to say, however, that everyone needs to get the better part of this education in schools as presently organized. At the moment, schools seem to most of us the best means for formal education of most people. Still, we need not reject totally those extreme critiques which call for the abolition of all schools.[31] It may be that these radical manifestoes are to be read as Rousseau wanted *Émile* to be understood—as indictments of social ills, serving to underscore reform proposals by provocative exaggeration.

Certainly there has always been dissatisfaction with schools because these institutions have always had their displeasing aspects. In the *Confessions* Augustine recalled how he crept to school hoping that today at least he might escape a beating. Comenius said that the schools of his time were slaughterhouses of the mind, and recent American critics have claimed that in our schools— urban or suburban, public and nonpublic—most children fail. In January 1969 a young woman reporter masqueraded as a student at Taft High School in the Bronx in order to collect material for a series in the *New York Post.* She sat in class one day next to a boy who confided that he hid his marijuana cigarettes in his socks because no one would look there even if he were searched on suspicion. When the reporter suggested that this was still a risky business, he simply said: "I couldn't stand this school if I wasn't stoned."

That incident in the Bronx may serve as a symbol of the bitter problems confronting some schools today and temper unrealistic theories. Such problems provoke two types of proposal for solution: reform or revolution. The reform effort is more common and strikes most people as the best line to take. It is what all the great figures in educational history tried to do: Isocrates, Quintilian,

Alcuin, Renaissance humanists like Vittorino da Feltre, the early Jesuit Schoolmen, Pestalozzi, Froebel, Montessori, Dewey, the American Progressivists, and their counterparts abroad like A. S. Neill. It means working to eliminate abuses and to recast and renew the whole school experience without blasting the entire enterprise to bits.

Reform will be fostered if we grant that education does not require the same number of years of schooling for everyone, even within the five-to-seventeen group. There are other agencies of education, after all. It is doubtful, for instance, if we learn as much in any five-year segment of schooling as we do from our parents in the first five years of life. Moreover, the years of schooling need not be consecutive for everyone. Any high school teacher knows that schooling for some teen-agers, at that point in their lives, is a waste if not a torment. But anyone who has lived to middle-life also knows that most people, including those who hated school at sixteen, have a certain desire to learn and to know something more about life than how to survive. It is worth weighing, therefore, some wise recommendations made by Margaret Mead long before the proposals to deschool society were announced.[32]

Writing in 1958 in the *Harvard Business Review,* Dr. Mead questioned the arrangement of American education. On the one hand, it keeps many young people in school much too long. On the other, it assumes that once school is finished, formal education is over. She suggested, then, that all children be given primary education but that, at fourteen or so, those not ready for continued academic work be allowed to take a job. Clearly this would require a reorganization of the work-world to make it physically and morally safe for the young people who chose to take this break in their schooling. But whenever they were ready to return to formal education, even if many years later, they should be encouraged to do so, and government monies should supply the equivalent of their salaries. It was because the anthropologist hoped to persuade industry to start such a program that she wrote in a magazine reaching business people. We cite her article not because its proposals are clearly practicable but because they show how to think about improving education by reforming schooling rather than by eliminating it.

CONTEMPLATION

Although the extension of humanistic culture to everyone is an aim of Catholic education, it is not its only aim nor the most characteristic. Every generous secular humanist will want to see all men educated to what Newman called intellectual excellence.

But there are two other goals that either go unnoticed in public schools or are not understood there as Christianity understands them. Catholics, however, should esteem these objectives as more important than other aspects of culture. It is possible to be a truly adult Christian without knowing much of art or science, but not without developing and uniting in one's life and person the two dimensions of *contemplation* and *work*. "Life," said Pius XII in the phrase used as an epigraph for this chapter, "is always a synthesis"; and contemplation and work are the prime elements it should combine. Each must be affirmed, and the harmony of the two should be realized by seeing the zone of work as ultimately instrumental in relation to the Reality toward which contemplation aspires. Let us say something about that contemplation here, speaking of work in the following chapter.

In the autumn of 1971 billboards in New York subway stations advertised a twelve-lecture evening course in "Practical Philosophy: For Clear Thought and Effective Action." A young man who took it said it was great—opened his eyes, changed his life. How? What did it teach that was so wonderful? Well, most importantly, how to be one with God. About this same time, the Sunday *New York Times* had accumulated so many new books dealing with the growing hunger for interiority, both in the Christian churches and outside them, that it packaged six for a single review. The reviewer remarked of the college students he knew: "They are turning inward, hoping to find some significance to life. They are attracted by the mysterious, the mystical, even the magical."[33]

There were plenty of other materials around demonstrating the extent of this interest among people at all ages. Sometimes it was being cultivated within the Christian tradition and sometimes by turning to Zen Buddhism or to yoga. But any Catholic whose memory reached back a quarter of a century did not need to be told that something new was abroad. His own knowledge of then and now was enough. Not that this was yet a mass movement nor free of ambiguities nor absolutely new. After all, the history of the Church could be written in terms of the shifting tides of concern for what devotional writers used to call the inner life of the Spirit. The agnostic historian may say that it only shows that when times are bad and people either despair of or are disgusted with the world, they go looking for union with God. The psychoanalyst may second this motion. But Christians can concede the analysis and still regard that motivation as a benefit of adversity—one more way in which all things work unto good.

In any case, as the 1960s ended and the 1970s began there were enough indications at hand to make a reader consider thoughtfully an essay written by E. I. Watkin in 1966. This distinguished member of the older generation of English Catholic intellectuals predicted that the Church was moving toward an era in which the spirit of Catholic Christianity would take precedence over the letter. And of this coming age he wrote: "A spiritual understanding, reserved hitherto for a minority of contemplatives, will be extended widely to all who without it would lose hold of religion altogether."[34]

These fragments are not cited to make an argument but to suggest that the forthcoming argument is neither so utopian nor so pietistic as it would have seemed a few decades ago. In 1972, for instance, a conference of Catholic Pentecostals drew 10,000 to the Notre Dame campus. The assertion that the Catholic community must aim at helping each of its members develop a genuine interior life would have to be made regardless of whether the climate were friendly or whether the Age of the Spirit were apparently on the horizon or still far off. But at the moment of this writing the claim can be made quite comfortably, is fashionable indeed!

We use the term *contemplation* deliberately because its very generality makes it possible to bundle three meanings into it. Christians should have some acquaintance with them all; from the Catholic standpoint, however, we shall be talking about two different orders of reality. Contemplation in the first sense is a natural activity, whereas contemplation in the third sense requires that accompanying divine assistance called grace. It belongs, in classical theological terminology, to the supernatural order. Contemplation in the second sense is usually understood by Catholics as a prayerful study which also presumes the presence of grace. A word about each of these.

Lewis Mumford remarked that Freud's studies of sexuality and Jung's studies of dreams and the unconscious were two complementary achievements that helped to reassert the inner life at a time when men had forgotten this better half of their world because of a rationalistic preoccupation with scientism and "dogmatic mechanistic doctrines."[35] Contemplation in the first of the senses intended here is another reassertion of that inward half of experience, this time from the side of the conscious, for it is a preeminent activity of the mind. To be sure it might well include within its purview the instructive data of psychoanalytic explorations. In the *Politics* Aristotle wrote that contemplation in this sense of philosophic reflection on the mysteries of life and being is the chief business of good citizens. Moreover, the chief business of the good state is to furnish an encouraging environment for this occupation. That contemplative habit of mind, so appropriate for all men, has always been honored by Christians and not least of all because it creates a disposition of receptivity for contemplation in the other two senses. Thus we find Vatican II sharing Mumford's concern and underlining the need to preserve, amid the dizzying expansion of specialized scientific knowledge, this "ability to contemplate and to wonder, from which wisdom comes."[36]

Thomas Aquinas, who was a good Aristotelian as well as a holy Christian, naturally enough, cordially esteemed contemplation, but he thought it should ideally be combined with service of others. For instance, he argued that the teacher's life, which unites study with helping the neighbor, is better than solitary reflection, just as to illuminate is better than simply to shine.[37] Besides, for Thomas the doing of metaphysics was the least part of contemplation. Far more important was contemplative study of divine things, especially as these are manifested in Christ and proclaimed in the scriptures. Indeed, all Christians would rank contemplation in this second sense ahead of the first. In Vatican II's "Dogmatic Constitution on Divine Revelation," usually recognized as one of the council's two most important productions, the bishops began by noting that God has revealed Himself both in His historic actions and in the scriptures recording these. The words proclaim the deeds; the deeds manifest and confirm the realities signified by the words. Thereafter the grasp of both realities and words grows in the religious society, the Church, "through the contemplation and study made by believers, who treasure these things in their hearts, through the intimate understanding of spiritual things they experience. . . ."[38]

Contemplation of the first two varieties requires leisure, and a certain amount of education helps. It was for these reasons, perhaps, that Plato and Aristotle assumed that working people have not the time, the taste, nor the aptitude for contemplative activities. But Christians judge the third kind of contemplation not only superior to the other two but possible and desirable for everyone (although having free time for it certainly makes it easier). This third type of contemplation is prayer in the purest sense of that word: a reverential and loving awareness of the presence of God, which is something quite different from mere philosophical thought about Him. By rights, this contemplation should be preeminent in the experience of every believer because the heart of Christian life is knowing and loving God, particularly in Christ, the Divine Word. Since there are no strict parallels for this knowledge, it can only be described as a quasi-experiential consciousness or an affective intuition of the Reality of God as present. The conventional and necessarily weak analogy is the example of a blindfolded man knowing that a friend sits wordlessly at his side. For many Christians, this prayer usually focuses on the Person of Jesus in and through Whom the mind and heart, to speak in human-wise, of God are known: "If you know me, you know my Father too" (John 14:7). It is the habit and practice of contemplation thus understood which the Catholic community must hope to see every man and woman attain. Yet the universality of this goal does not generally seem to have been acknowledged or pursued the way universal literacy has been.

It could be, though. This is not the exceptional prayer of gifted mystics like Paul and Teresa of Avila. It does not require affluent leisure, theological sophistication, or the monastic milieu. It has often been realized by people who were poor, relatively uneducated, and endlessly busy making a living. In one of his studies on mysticism, Maréchal spoke movingly of an old peasant woman sitting at her fireside after a long day in the fields, gently caught up in a profound affective awareness of God's presence as she recited her rosary. Robert Coles's reports of his talk with migrant workers and the urban poor confirm this example with contemporary factual data. A woman who worked all week picking beans told him: "I've got myself rested and strong now, because God will refresh you, if you ask Him, if you only ask Him. I'll be talking with the Lord, and all of a sudden I know He's touched me and given me a little of His strength, so I can go on."[39] And in Boston a woman recalled earlier days in the South: "It used to be in Waycross, Georgia, I'd sit in church for hours and we could have a good long talk for ourselves, God and me, and God and my sister."[40]

One of the oldest Christian descriptions of this prayer is still one of the best. Attributed to various shadowy fifth-century churchmen, it calls prayer the *anabasis,* or the mounting-upward of the mind to God—where "mind" is to be understood as mind and heart together. This ascent can be the inner side of several different kinds of worship. But we are not speaking here primarily either of the recitation of prayer-formulas or even of Catholicism's public worship, the Eucharistic liturgy. Surely neither of these is to be devaluated. The formulas, after all, include the Lord's Own Prayer, and any of them may awaken that sense of the divine presence if said with devout attention. The liturgy, moreover, effects a unique union with God by, as Catholics believe, making Christ really present beneath the appearances of the sacramental gifts of bread and wine. Vatican II said of this great cultive act: "No other action of the Church can match its claim to efficacy, nor equal the degree of it."[41]

But on the whole, the Church and its leadership have not

neglected this liturgy nor failed to make its benefits available for all the Catholic people. Over the centuries the Mass has been a form of significant religious experience and education for each generation. In the great cathedrals all the resources of architecture, music, painting and sculpture, sacred furnishings, and splendid ritual combined to deepen that sense of the mystery and majesty of God evoked by this liturgy. But even in poor little country churches, worshippers could be caught up in the twofold rhythm of the Mass: the offering of themselves along with the gifts, and the coming of the Lord to them after those gifts had been consecrated. Without explicity saying so to themselves, these people actually experienced the "way by which the Christian liturgy embodies concretely the essential meaning of education from a Christian perspective."[42]

It is true that the liturgical framework of the central action has constantly to be updated; but the very vigor and success of the twentieth-century liturgical reform proves that the public cult has been taken seriously. Some critics, in fact, have complained that the liturgy has been too much emphasized at the expense of a concern for social justice. In any case, the liturgical forms of yesterday, when reasonably well done, awakened that sense of the Holy and an appreciation of the Eucharist as a sacrifice and a communion with Christ. The newer forms create more effectively a sense of community among the worshippers and an appreciation of the Eucharist as a sacred meal nourishing their fellowship. Perhaps tomorrow an ideal form will emerge successfully uniting both these dimensions. Here let us simply note that the importance of the public worship has been adequately acknowledged and does not need to be underscored.

But the possibility and the desirability of all Christians developing that inner, contemplative dimension of true prayer does seem to call for emphasis. The council itself, in its document on the liturgy, also observed that men's religious experience is not confined to their participation in the public cult. "The Christian is assuredly called to pray with his brethren, but he must also enter into his chamber to pray to the Father in secret; indeed, according to the teaching of the Apostle Paul, he should pray without ceasing."[43]

No doubt if Christians are to speak exactly they will not say that either the basic disposition to inwardness and prayer or the actual awareness of God can be taught in the strict sense, for these are gifts of grace. Indeed, even naturally good dispositions cannot be taught in the literal sense of that word. Plato, to be sure, seems to have thought they could; but Aristotle disagreed, and experience sides with Aristotle. In the geometry class the student is taught when he is brought to see for himself that two parallel lines never meet in the Euclidean universe. The same pupil could be conducted to a theoretical appreciation of the nature, necessity, and beauty of truthfulness; yet that does not insure his honesty. But he might be provided with surroundings and personal examples that would accustom him to acting honestly and developing an esteem for that moral disposition.

So too there are methods for disposing oneself for prayerful contemplation which can be described and then practiced: the cultivation of quiet within and without; reading the Gospels meditatively; learning to sound one's own depths and to listen. Nowadays we hear a good deal about the methods of Zen Buddhism or yoga, and we might remember that the Christian tradition has its own rich fund of teachings about procedures for recollection and prayer. What remains, however, is to find ways of making this tradition available for everyone. It is important that this education to the interior life of the Spirit take place well within the community of faith which is the Church. For in this way it will more easily avoid the dangers of extravagance, extreme subjectivism, and illuminism.

If the disposition we have been calling contemplation were to be widely cultivated, the benefits would be both individual and social. There would be benefits for the individual, because in prayer the person experiences his own truest self as well as that quasi-immediate encounter with God—indeed, because of that encounter. Prayer is, in the first place, man's response to God's imprescriptable right to adoration; but it is also the discovery of friendship with Him and a progressive understanding of what His will for us may be. The self of which we become aware in this meeting is not the self of that swarm of anxieties about life and work, about personal relationships, failures, temptations, and frustrations, which so often buzz through consciousness when we pray; rather, it is the deep-down subject which knows these experiences but is not identified with them. At the close of her greatest novel, Willa Cather had the dying archbishop reflect that life is an experience of the Ego but not the Ego itself. It is that true Ego that comes to know itself fully in responding to the invitation to address God as *Thou*: "Our Father, Who art in heaven, hallowed be Thy name. . . ." Saint Paul sometimes spoke of the *pneuma* or spirit, an element beyond both flesh and psyche. Without presuming to interpret this usage we might borrow it and say that in prayer the human spirit becomes aware not only of God but of itself. "I reckon myself blessed, Lord, and highly blessed, if I feel you with me," wrote William of St. Thierry in a twelfth-century treatise on contemplation. "As long as I am with you, I am also with myself; I am no longer myself when I am not with you."[44]

But this awareness is more than marvelously instructive and restorative for the individual. If a vast community of men and women were to achieve this interiority, that would itself be the source of exceptional solidarity among them. Where such solidarity existed, there would be the best of foundations for concerted action in the world and the best of hopes for its success. In the final chapter, we shall say something about the character of that Christian social action.

NOTES

1. Saint Thomas Aquinas, *Summa Thelogiae,* I–II, q. 94, a. 2, c.
2. "Man's social nature makes it evident that the progress of the human person and the advance of society itself hinge on each other. For the beginning, the subject and the goal of all social institutions is and must be the human person, which for its part and by its very nature stands completely in need of social life. This social life is not something added on to man. Hence, through his dealings with others, through reciprocal duties, and through fraternal dialogue he develops all his gifts and is able to rise to his destiny." From the "Pastoral Constitution on the Church in the Modern World," quoted from the English translation of *The Documents of Vatican II,* Walter M. Abbott, S.J., gen. ed. (New York: Guild-America-Association Presses, 1966), n. 25, p. 224. In the decades just before the council, these themes were profoundly developed by such distinguished Catholic thinkers as Jacques Maritain, in *Integral Humanism,* and the great Italian priest, sociologist, and founder in 1919 of the "Popular Party," Don Luigi Sturzo, in *The Inner Laws of Society.*
3. Pius XII, "The Unity of Human Society" (*Summi Pontificatus*), *The Catholic Mind,* 37 (November 1939), 912. The document was issued October 20, 1939.
4. From a talk given January 31, 1971, and quoted in *L'Osservatore Romano,* weekly English edition, February 4, 1971, p. 12.
5. John Dewey, *Democracy and Education* (New York: Macmillan, 1916), p. 417.
6. Ronald Blythe, *Akenfield: Portrait of an English Village* (New York: Pantheon, 1969), pp. 163–164. To the point also are these comments

by R. S. Peters, one of the leading English philosophers of education: "I am haunted by what people are making of their lives; what they are doing and where they are going. . . . Education is the initiation into worthwhile activities." Barry Hill, "Professor Richard Peters, The Practical Philosopher," *The Times Educational Supplement,* March 5, 1971, p. 11.

7. Paul VI, *Populorum Progressio* ("On the Development of Peoples"), Encyclical Letter of March 26, 1967, quoted here from the text as given in the *New York Times,* March 29, 1967, p. 23.

8. Cardinal Suenens, *The Nun in the World,* trans. Geoffrey Stevens (Westminster, Ind.: Newman Press, 1962), p. 150.

9. These are basic Christian themes and they are often invoked by the documents of Vatican II. But the appeal to them here was suggested by the text of a remarkable BBC talk by R. W. Southern, Professor of Modern History at Oxford: "Religious Humanism," *The Listener,* 75 (August 26, 1965), 303–305.

10. This formulation was suggested by a page of Don Sturzo and by a line in an essay by an American interpreter of his thought. See Luigi Sturzo, *Inner Laws of Society: A New Sociology,* trans. Barbara Barclay Carter (New York: Kenedy, 1944), p. xiv; and Robert C. Pollock, "History is a Matrix," *Thought,* 26 (Summer 1951), 207.

11. These paragraphs draw freely on some pages in the author's *St. Thomas Aquinas and Education* (New York: Random House, 1968), pp. 64–67.

12. *New York Herald-Tribune,* September 21, 1959, p. 1.

13. Pierre Rousselot, "Amour spirituel et Synthèse aperceptive," *Revue de Philosophie,* 16 (March 1910), 225–240.

14. Saint Thomas Aquinas, *Summa contra Gentiles,* IV, c. 11.

15. The suggestion made by Anthony T. Padovano in his lucid and instructive account of current theological reflection on Original Sin, *Original Sin and Christian Anthropology* (Washington: Corpus Books, 1969), pp. 23–25.

16. Cyril Vollert, S.J., "Original Sin and Education," *Review for Religious,* 5 (July 1946), 219. For a misunderstanding of the doctrine of Original Sin which supposes it to mean that man is essentially evil, see Anne Roe, *The Making of a Scientist* (New York: Dodd, Mead, 1952), p. 241.

17. "Pastoral Constitution on the Church in the Modern World," *The Documents of Vatican II, op. cit.,* n. 31, p. 229.

18. This analysis of teaching is found in the eleventh of Saint Thomas Aquinas' *Quaestiones disputatae de Veritate* ("Academic Disputations concerning Truth") and a translation of it by James V. McGlynn, S.J., has been issued as *Thomas Aquinas: The Teacher* (Chicago: Regnery, 1954).

19. "Declaration on Christian Education" (October 28, 1965), English translation of *The Documents of Vatican II,* Walter M. Abbott, S.J., gen. ed. (New York: Guild-America-Association Presses, 1966), n. 3, p. 641.
20. *Meyer* v. *Nebraska,* 262 U.S. 400.
21. *Pierce* v. *Society of Sisters, Pierce* v. *Hill Military Academy,* 268 U.S. 535.
22. "Declaration on the Relationship of the Church to Non-Christian Religions" (October 28, 1965), *The Documents of Vatican II, op. cit.,* n. 5, p. 668.
23. What is the actual content of this "culture"? No doubt, that will be differently defined from place to place and epoch to epoch. However, the document quoted here, the "Pastoral Constitution on the Church in the Modern World," lists three focal categories: "Man judges rightly that by his intellect he surpasses the material universe, for he shares in the light of the divine mind. By relentlessly employing his talents through the ages, he has indeed made progress in the practical sciences, technology, and the liberal arts" *The Documents of Vatican II, op. cit.,* n. 15, pp. 212–213. The commission which recommended in 1964 the establishment of a National Humanities Foundation as a counterbalance to the National Science Foundation (the National Endowment for the Humanities was the result) defined those nonscientific humanities to include languages, literature, history, philosophy, the study of the history, theory and criticism of art and music, the history and comparative study of religion, and law. If theology and the physical and social sciences are added to these, we have a working description for specification of culture in the fullness of the sense in which the term is used here.
24. John Dewey, *The School and Society,* rev. ed. (Chicago: University of Chicago Press, 1943), p. 7.
25. "Pastoral Constitution on the Church in the Modern World," *The Documents of Vatican II, op. cit.,* n. 9, p. 207 and n. 60, p. 267. See also the "Declaration on Christian Education," *ibid.,* n. 1, p. 639.
26. Quoted in Louis R. Harlan, *Separate and Unequal: Public School Campaigns and Racism in the Southern Seaboard States 1901–1915* (Chapel Hill: University of North Carolina Press, 1958), p. 102.
27. Thomas Jefferson, *Notes on the State of Virginia,* edited with an introduction and notes by William Peden (Chapel Hill: University of North Carolina Press, 1955), p. 146. The first authorized edition of Jefferson's *Notes* appeared in 1787.
28. *General Education in a Free Society: Report of the Harvard Committee* (Cambridge: Harvard University Press, 1948), p. 51.
29. James B. Conant, "Vocational Education and the National Need," *American Vocational Journal,* 35 (January, 1960), 15–19.

30. Lorenzo K. Reed, S.J., "Excellence for Whom?" *National Catholic Educational Association Bulletin,* 57 (August 1960), 267–272.
31. See Ivan Illich, *Deschooling Society* (New York: Harper & Row, 1971), and Everett W. Reimer, *School Is Dead* (Garden City, N.Y.: Doubleday, 1971).
32. Margaret Mead, "Thinking Ahead: Why Is Education Obsolete?" *Harvard Business Review,* 36 (November–December 1958), 23–37, 164–170.
33. Chad Walsh, *New York Times Book Review,* November 28, 1971, p. 46.
34. E. I. Watkin, "The Wisdom of the Spirit: A Platonist's Faith," in Michael de la Bedoyere, ed., *The Future of Catholic Christianity* (Philadelphia: Lippincott, 1966), p. 312. For an example of the wonderfully learned skepticism that links interest in union with God to despair of the word, see E. R. Dodds, *Pagan and Christian in an Age of Anxiety: Some Aspects of Religious Experience from Marcus Aurelius to Constantine* (Cambridge: at the University Press, 1965).
35. Lewis Mumford, "Books: The Revolt of the Demons," *The New Yorker,* 40 (May 23, 1964), 155–185.
36. "Pastoral Constitution on the Church in the Modern World," *The Documents of Vatican II, op. cit.,* n. 56, p. 261.
37. Saint Thomas Aquinas, *Summa Theologiae,* II–II, q. 188, a. 6, c.
38. "Dogmatic Constitution on Divine Revelation," *The Documents of Vatican II, op. cit.,* n. 8, p. 116.
39. Robert Coles, "Talking with God," *Commonweal,* 91 (December 12, 1969), 332.
40. Robert Coles, "The Lord of the Ghettos," *Commonweal,* 92 (November 13, 1970), 171.
41. "Constitution on the Sacred Liturgy," *The Documents of Vatican II, op. cit.,* n. 7, p. 141.
42. Massey H. Shepherd, Jr., "The Liturgy and Christian Education," in Edmund Fuller, ed., *The Christian Idea of Education* (New Haven: Yale University Press, 1957), p. 125.
43. "Constitution on the Sacred Liturgy," *The Documents of Vatican II, op. cit.,* n. 12, p. 143.
44. From "Meditation Two," in *The Works of William of St. Thierry,* Vol. I, *On Contemplating God—Prayer—Meditations,* trans. Sister Penelope, CSMV (Spencer, Mass.: Cistercian Publications, 1971), n. 2, pp. 95–96.

Toward Transformation of the World: The Social Goals of Catholic Education

> We are witnesses of the birth of a new humanism, one in which man is defined first of all by his responsibility toward his brothers and toward history.
>
> *Vatican II*
> *"The Church in the Modern World," n. 55*

Paul VI, receiving the day's visitors to Saint Peter's in June 1970, remarked: "Religious life cannot be practised as an individualistic expression of the relations between man and God. The spirit of community is the atmosphere necessary for the believer."[1] No doubt the Pope was thinking of the Church community in the first place; but since a believer is a man before he is a Christian, the application of his words can be extended to include all the other fundamental human communities.

A believer's relationship to these communities must be reciprocal. Not only does he need them but they need him. They cannot constitute even a minimal human environment unless a sufficient number of their members contribute a rational and responsible service sufficient to hold back anarchy. Christians, then, do well to think about human nature's social dimension and its consequent obligations. In doing so they will necessarily draw on the same three sources consulted by Christian schoolmen when they try to comprehend the total work of education in the real world. In the first place, specific problems require concrete solutions, which the social sciences can do a great deal to fashion but which experience alone can validate. Intelligent designing of these techniques, however, presupposes a theoretical–practical framework provided by political and social philosophies. These philosophies, in turn, are reenforced and enlarged by a few evangelical principles that do not supplant sound social doctrine but complement it.

It was noted in the first chapter that these pages do not represent an attempt to outline solutions for current school problems or even a complete educational theory congenial to Catholics. We try simply to sketch that portion of such a theory which is distilled from the Gospel message as this is understood within Catholicism. The aim of this final chapter must be similarly limited. There is no intention either of condensing the substance of a social philosophy consonant with the pertinent teachings of Catholicism or of prescribing remedies for the awesome social sicknesses of our time. Every Christian must, according to his abilities and opportunities, relate his faith to his community experience and the needs of the societies within which he lives. Some of these Christians will be social philosophers or social scientists. Some will have the chance and duty to work up precedures for social improvement, for bringing about what the Bishops' Synod of 1971 repeatedly called the "transformation of the world."[2] All will have the chance and opportunity to make some contribution to this effort at transformation, this task, as Vatican II put it, "of constructing for all men everywhere a world more genuinely human."[3]

Christians will be more likely to join in this effort if they have absorbed two convictions, grounded on the Gospel and converted by the believers into habitual and effective moral dispositions. For the impact of these understandings, attitudes, and habits is predominantly social, although naturally they also shape and color individual personal experience. Growth along these lines constitutes two broad social goals which Catholic education should consistently promote through the family, through the ministry of the Word (for instance, preaching during liturgies) and through formal and informal education within the Catholic school. The first of these convictions is that human work and the whole collective effort at civilization it supports are true values that Christians should acknowledge and serve. The second principle is that this collective effort, as well as each individual's share in it, should be directed toward creating a really humane, just social environment for all people everywhere, even as it contributes to the individual maturation of those participating in this enterprise. Let us first say something about each of these focal ideals and then wind this book up with a brief coda on the school as one of the chief instruments now at hand for institutionalizing the effort to realize both the individual and the social goals of Christian education.

TWO STRANDS IN THE
CHRISTIAN VIEW OF THE WORLD

. . . the expectation of a new earth must not weaken but rather stimulate our concern for cultivating this one.

Vatican II
"The Church in the Modern World," n. 39

It is easy enough to enunciate the foregoing social goals, but can they also be defended as distinctively Christian? In this whole notion of a Christian humanism is there not a tension that cannot be uprooted? Does not any real humanism require a commitment to earthly values—whereas, if Christians agree with Saint Paul that their "homeland is in heaven," must they not conclude with Newman: "This is the legitimate use of this world, to make us seek for another."[4] As far as Christian education goes, perhaps the devout Amish people are right. They work hard. Their farms are productive even though the Amish abjure sophisticated machinery. Their family life is warm and secure despite a certain austerity. But they reject most of contemporary civilization's spectacular flowerings in technology and the arts and sciences. They have often collided with heavy-handed bureaucrats because they do not allow their children to go to any school beyond the eighth grade and preferably not to public schools at all. As one Amish father put it: "We don't want our children involved in worldly things. In the public schools they have physical education, science, television, things like that—temptations for a different world." Predictably enough, this outlook disenchants the neighbors, and an Iowan real estate man grumbled that the Amish "just don't buy things that everybody else buys."[5]

But we should not conclude too promptly that the Amish have got Christianity all wrong. They have at least clearly understood one of the two main strands in its complex doctrine about this world. That is the call for detachment, which must be combined with the call for involvement. The tension between these two central elements in the Christian ideal attitude has necessarily been examined by every distinguished writer on Christian humanism. Newman spoke to the issue more than once in *The Idea of a University.* In *We Hold These Truths* John Courtney Murray, S.J., devoted the chapter entitled "Is It Basket Weaving?" to what he called the question of Christianity and human values. Here we describe quite briefly those two themes and suggest how they may be brought together in a true unity.

The Amish speak for a solid tradition running back to the century of Christian origins. Its existence scarcely needs demonstrating, since it is commonly acknowledged (although in no danger of being overemphasized today). We might line up, however, a few emblematic texts to illustrate the tendency that in recent decades has been labeled *eschatological* because it accents the end of time and the realities lying beyond the final horizon—the *eschata* or last things. The Lord did, after all, command His followers to seek first the Kingdom of God and not to worry about food and shelter. The Letter to the Hebrews has a ringing phrase echoing this motif and praising the patriarchs for having understood that they were only pilgrims and strangers on earth.

Every Christian ponders this reminder, at least once in awhile; and often the gifted spirits and those of widest experience respond to it most strongly. In third-century North Africa, the brilliant and vehement Tertullian declared roundly: "We have no concern in this life except to depart from it as speedily as possible."[6] This highly educated man, who had already appropriated the best secular culture of his day, also said: "After Jesus Christ we have no need of speculation, after the Gospel no need of research."[7] Augustine phrased this viewpoint and emotion with greater nuance when he observed in the *Confessions* that man's soul, in whatever direction it turns and toward whatever beautiful things, will only be filled with sorrow if it fixes on anything other than God. Saint Peter Damian, who lived not in the civilized Mediterranean world but in the rough eleventh century, was fiercely antihumanistic; he announced that he spurned Plato and Euclid alike and would be instructed only by the simplicity of Christ.

The Imitation of Christ, a fifteenth-century devotional book for lay people, made the same point with greater tranquillity: "He to whom the eternal Word speaks, what need has he of genera and species." And Newman, addressing the secure and complacent segment of nineteenth-century England, summoned his Oxford congregation to Christian otherworldiness:

It is religion itself which we all by nature dislike, not the excess merely. Nature tends toward the earth, and God is in heaven . . . We must, at least at seasons, defraud ourselves of nature, if we would not be defrauded of grace . . . Let us look forward to the time when this world will have passed away and all its delusions; and when we, when every one born of woman, must either be in heaven or in hell.[8]

Or as John XXIII said opening the Second Vatican Council on October 11, 1962, since we are pilgrims on earth, our lives must "be ordered in such a way as to fulfill our duties as citizens of earth and heaven, and thus to attain the aim of life as established by God."

For the fully rounded Catholic view of human work and secular culture, however, we must synthesize this concept of otherworldiness and detachment with a different but equally authentic element. That amounts to an affirmation of those same earthly values which Tertullian could not abide. The Master also taught the parable of talents, and since Christians are supposed to relieve poverty and suffering, it may be concluded that among the talents to be developed are those natural gifts whereby the earth is humanized and its resources cultivated for the benefit of all. Paul not only told the Philippians that their *politeuma* was heaven, but he also thanked them for their gifts of money and recommended that they fill their minds with everything true and lovely or gracious and worthy of praise. This too became part of the tradition; and the second-century writer and martyr Justin said: "The truths which men in all lands have rightly spoken belong to us Christians."

The practical significance of this conviction was instructively grasped in third-century Alexandria. That cosmopolitan Egyptian trading city was the hub of Greek, Oriental, and Roman influences; an intellectual as well as a business center that forcibly confronted Christians with the need for working out a harmony between the halves of their twofold vocation as "citizens of earth and heaven." So it was not surprising that the first full-bodied example of a Christian humanism was created here by two great teachers, the Greek Clement (c. 150–215) and his Egyptian successor Origen (c. 185–253). They aimed to synthesize *pistis* and *sophia,* faith and secular culture, in their students' persons. To promote this, they provided a curriculum in which studies in Greek philosophy and science were carried on in an atmosphere of complete intellectual freedom as a preparation for the crowning study of theology. Clement had two attractive images for this ideal of synthesis. In *Exhortation to the Greeks,* he imagined the enlightened pagan philosophers and poets joining the congregation of believers, which resembles an orchestra in which many different instruments are melodiously united under the direction of Christ the Word. And in the *Miscellanies* (*Stromata,* 1, 5) he remarked that the river of truth is one, although fed by many streams.

This persuasion that Christians should properly honor and participate in all the arts and sciences, in works of technology, speculation, and exploration, has a certain base in Catholic faith. From the belief in God's assumption of human nature in the Incarnation of the Word, it has been concluded that all authentic human goods have been ratified and enhanced. They have all been caught up in the saving life and work of the Lord and make their own contribution to the transcendent destiny of man. Other things being equal, the savage is a poorer candidate for sanctity than the person of civilized mind and heart; people who are deprived of life's necessities, moreover, hardly have time for mysticism. Thus in every age, spokesmen for the Christian mainstream have defended what is nowadays called the Incarnational emphasis. In the medieval world, for instance, it was not just that a Thomas Aquinas used Greek philosophy to do theology and a Dante created epic Catholic poetry. The Church was then the ordinary welfare agency and a chief patron of the arts; even Saint Bernard, who usually took a dim view of cultural pursuits, wrote books and founded monasteries where the monks created fertile farms and austerely beautiful cloisters.

But if Catholic Christianity, as a whole, has always understood that its humanism and education must weave together these strands of detachment and involvement, it has been during the past hundred years, particularly, that the more emphatic affirmation of earthly values has been made, with the popes as leading witnesses. Naturally enough, both the eschatological and the incarnational stresses were kept in focus. Tertullian and Bernard would have been quite comfortable with Leo XIII's saying in *Rerum Novarum,* his 1891 encyclical on the dignity and rights of labor, that "the things of earth cannot be understood or valued aright without taking into consideration the life to come."[9] But we cannot imagine their saying, as Leo did in the encyclical on the Christian constitution of states, that

[The Church] will always encourage and promote, as she does in other branches of knowledge, all study occupied with the investigation of nature. . . . She never objects to search being made for things that minister to the refinements and comforts of life. So far, indeed, from opposing these she is now, as she ever has been, hostile alone to indolence and sloth, and earnestly wishes that the talents of men may bear more and more abundant fruit by cultivation and exercise.[10]

Pius XI, who was both director of the Vatican Library and an ardent alpinist, was equally removed from the obscurantism of Peter Damian and the rather too worldly humanism of his Renaissance predecessor, Aeneas Silvius. "The Church," Pius XI said on one occasion, "has always considered it her duty to assist and promote the cultivation of human arts and disciplines."[11] And in his encyclical on Christian education he noted succinctly that such education "aims at securing the Supreme Good, that is, God, for the souls of those who are being educated and the maximum of well-being possible here below for human society."[12]

But it remained for Eugenio Pacelli, Pius XII, to acknowledge time and again during his long reign not merely the usefulness but the intrinsic value of the whole vast creative and demiurgic human enterprise. We could cite hundreds of passages from the enormous deposit of his writings, but here there is only room for two typical ones. "The Church loves and favors human progress," he said in his Christmas Eve Address of 1953. Then he went on to praise technology:

"Inhabit the earth and subject it" (Genesis 1:28) said God to man as He handed creation over to him in temporary heritage. What a long and hard road from then to the present day, when men can at last say that they have in some measure fulfilled the divine command. . . . Now it is clear that all search for and discovery of the forces of nature, which technology effectuates, is at once a search for and discovery of the greatness, of the wisdom and of the harmony of God.[13]

And once, speaking to a group of secondary school teachers, he warned them "against a blind attachment to the past which would today frustrate the efficacy of your work." Their goal, he said, ought to be the education of a perfect Christian and he added: "By the perfect Christian we mean the Christian of today, child of his own era, knowing and cultivating all the advances made by science and technical skill; a citizen and not something apart from the life led in his own country today."[14]

Now Pius XII, as commentators have noted, was one of the great teachers of the bishops at Vatican II, and their conciliar documents often refer to items from the immense corpus of his almost twenty years of papal utterances. Very likely the bishops found those writings congenial because they too were engaged in the intellectual task of working out the implications of this Catholic conviction that the authentically human and the authentically Christian are ordered to each other in a harmonious relationship. In fact, the "Pastoral Constitution on the Church in the Modern World" affirmed that world so vigorously that a Protestant reader, Robert McAfee Brown, felt it was rather overdone and thought the eschatological aspect needed more development.[15] In any case, the council's teaching should have dissolved the misapprehension that Catholic Christianity sees an essential division between the concept of a good Christian and the concept of a responsible world citizen.

Here, in a single passage from the Pastoral Constitution are the three key ideas that can effect a synthesis of the concepts of detachment and involvement: (1) Mankind's true fulfillment is said to be reached only at the end of time, but (2) it begins even now for the values of this life are intrinsically good (indeed, in some mysterious fashion material creation will itself be redeemed); and (3) at the same time, all these values are understood to have an instrumental and dispositive role for the attaining of that Age-to-Come.

We do not know the time for the consummation of the earth and of humanity. Nor do we know how all things will be transformed. As deformed by sin, the shape of this world will pass away. But we are taught that God is preparing a new dwelling place and a new earth where justice will abide, and whose blessedness will answer and surpass all the longings for peace which spring up in the human heart. . . . Therefore, while we are warned that it profits a man nothing if he gain the whole world and lose himself, the expectation of a new earth must not weaken but rather stimulate our concern for cultivating this one. For here grows the body of a new human family, a body which even now is able to give some kind of foreshadowing of the new age.

Earthly progress must be carefully distinguished from the growth of Christ's kingdom. Nevertheless, to the extent that the former can contribute to the better ordering of human society, it is of vital concern to the kingdom of God.

For after we have obeyed the Lord, and in His Spirit nurtured on earth the values of human dignity, brotherhood and freedom, and indeed all the good fruits of our nature and enterprise, we will find then again, but freed of stain, burnished and transfigured.[16]

If this medley of texts were supposed to constitute an argument, it could be objected that a Cook's tour cannot do the job of a geodetic survey. But these two basic Christian themes have only been counterpointed to bring a question into strong relief. For it is not really necessary to prove that the many-stranded Catholic attitude toward time and the world requires allegiance to both those tendencies. The specialist in Church history knows this, and so does the ordinary Catholic. The great prayers of the liturgy ask one Sunday for temporal benefits such as health; on another, they ask that amid the changes of this world, the hearts of believers may always be fixed on their true felicity; on a third Sunday, we pray that Christians may use the good things of this life in a way that does not cause them to lose eternal life. It is true that some contemporary Catholic writers are outraged by those last two petitions and would have them thrown out. But they cannot be discarded without rejecting half the truth. For if we ask which of these contrasting attitudes is genuinely Christian—that of involved concern for the world and that of detachment from it—the answer is unequivocal, however hard to reduce to practice. Both attitudes are essential. To emphasize one at the expense of the other is a perennial temptation; yielding to it is a betrayal. We must avoid both a Buddhistic withdrawal from the world and a naturalistic idolization of it. We must neither despise human powers nor rely on them exclusively. Life, for the Christian, must always be a synthesis, since it must always be, as the classic phrase has it, a combination of opposites: *compositio oppositorum.*

This is true, in the first place, in the distinctively supernatural order, the life of grace. The New Testament makes this clear, for it underscores the tension evoked because the Reign of God is *now* here but *not yet* in its fullness. "My dear people," says Saint John, "we are already the children of God but what we are to be in the future has not yet been revealed" (1 John 3:2).[17] Since grace transforms and elevates nature but neither destroys nor negates it, it is not surprising to find a similar tension running throughout the natural order and requiring the resolution of a number of apparent antinomies. Time and eternity, the sacred and the profane, the person and the community, the civic commonwealth and the Church, action and contemplation, freedom and responsibility—in each case it is necessary to affirm both elements and to unify them in life itself, so that they coexist in a harmony that overcomes contrasts and oppositions without destroying either of two complementary values or dissolving them both into a lifeless mix.

Irving Babbitt (1865–1932), who considered himself the humanistic apostle of "poised and proportionate" living along lines laid down by Confucius, Aristotle, and some of the Renaissance figures, once cited approvingly Luther's comparison of mankind to a drunken peasant on horseback who, if propped up on one side, slumps over on the other. Babbitt thought that this represented what always happens in the history of thought, and he himself was continually running from one side to the other trying to overcome "the indolence of extremes." To state the Catholic view fairly, we must overcome any similar laziness, acknowledging that since Christians are complex beings in a complex universe, their response to the world must be corresponding complex—a combination, if you like, of Augustine and Teilhard, of the *Imitation of Christ* and Bonhoeffer's "Letters from Prison."

How will such a synthesis be conceived in theory and lived in practice? It cannot be brought about merely by placing the two elements inertly side by side. For any synthesis must combine its parts into a new, complex but real whole. When the term is used in chemistry, for instance, "synthesis" describes the formation of an organic compound whose heterogeneous parts are so united that each contributes to the making of the new thing and exercises its functions for the good of that whole. The combining of hydrogen and oxygen produces water, and this example suggests the character of any real synthesis.

The Christian will not achieve that synthesis if he eliminates one of its elements so as to make all temporal realities sacred or all of them secular. It is not enough to judge the world valuable *only* because it is a sign pointing toward God. For this view fails to appreciate sufficiently that inherent goodness of creation which Vatican II acknowledged when it recognized the relative "autonomy of earthly affairs" stemming from the truth "that created things and societies themselves enjoy their own laws and values which must be gradually deciphered, put to use, and regulated by men."[18] And, of course, neither would synthesis be obtained by thinking that the sole reason for esteeming the world is that it is good and beautiful in itself and totally independent of the Gospel. The classic Catholic way of harmonizing the sacred and the secular—the concern, to use Vatican II's terms, for the temporal sphere with the concern for the eternal vocation—is to see the secular realm both as intrinsically worthwhile and as a means or instrument for achieving that union with God in Jesus Christ which the Gospel proclaims as the purpose of life. This is both a theoretical and practical recipe for a true synthesis because the two realities are now functionally related to one another as a means is to an end; thus they constitute a new whole.

Men and women could not consume their lives in their various roles of parents, farmers and artisans, scientists and artists, business people and professionals, if they were not sustained by an insight into the intrinsic value of all the endeavors that build and sustain the human communities. But if they are Christians, they will also know that within the larger perspective these excellences appear as intermediate goods, having the quality both of a goal and a factor. As Aquinas put it: "Among objects in themselves lovable, some are loved solely for themselves and never for anything else—thus happiness which is the last end—while others are loved both for their own sake, in that they possess some intrinsic worth, and also because they serve the purpose of conveying us to a more perfect good—thus are the virtues lovable."[19] A man or a woman is more than parent or worker and his or her life is not comprehended by the vocation or the career. In the final reckoning, the whole realm of temporal activity is ordered as a means to a transcendent and absolute value. John XXIII made that point in one of the great Christian humanistic documents of our time, *Mater et Magistra* ("Christianity and Social Progress"):

Certainly, the Church has always taught and continues to teach that scientific and technical progress and the resultant material well-being are truly good and, as such, must be regarded as an important sign of progress in human civilization. Nevertheless, in the Church's view, these things should be valued according to their true worth: i.e., as means for achieving more effectively a higher end—that of facilitating and promoting a man's perfection, both in the natural and the supernatural order.[20]

A CHRISTIAN VIEW OF WORK

The general Christian esteem for earthly values has a particular application for each individual person and that, in turn, has specific implications for education. Since it is chiefly through their occupations that people share in the collective effort to build rational, humane societies, the lives of Christians must combine the action of work with the contemplation described in the preceding chapter. Here again the distinctive and only acceptable goal is that of a true synthesis.

It follows, therefore, that the total education of men and women must include education for and through work. Even the period of general schooling does not teach how to live as a lesson sharply distinguished from how to make a living, although this catchword may be dusted off annually at commencement time. But in fact a great deal of general education is actually vocational, even if that purpose is veiled and assumes forms more subtle than direct job training. Many Americans go on to high school or college precisely in order to be eligible for better employment. Their expectations have usually not been disappointed, although an oversupply of college graduates may yet scramble this pattern. On the other hand, vocational preparation, whether narrow or broad, is not the only possible link between the areas of work and education. Work might be defined as the expenditure of spiritual and bodily energies for the support and enhancement of life. But since many work activities have a distinctive intellectual and moral value, some of them can be made available to children at home or in school precisely for the sake of these benefits and quite independently of their economic function. Moreover, if work and contemplation are chief components of a complete life, then it is at least desirable that home, church, and school equip youth with a philosophical and theological appreciation of labor's worth.[21]

A good deal was done in the decades preceding Vatican II, particularly by Belgian, French and German writers, to develop a "theology of work," and the council profited from these reflections and gave their conclusions wider currency. These conclusions are chiefly three and flow from the effort to discover, as it were, God's view of human work by reflection on the divine action manifested in Creation, in the Incarnation, and in the bestowal of grace. God is understood, in the first place, to intend man's work as a fully natural and desirable expression of human powers. Work is neither a curse nor an accident. Since the earth comes from God, it is good, and so is the work which develops it properly. Indeed, Paul said that the material world can itself look for salvation: "Creation still retains the hope of being freed, like us, from its slavery to decadence, to enjoy the same freedom and glory as the Children of God" (Romans 8:21).

Second, God is seen as intending work to be one of the means for building up our psychological personality and our moral character in both their natural and supernatural dimensions. Third, work is also a means whereby we support the whole network of human societies: family and church, town, state, and nation, and all the smaller groups organized for business, service, or recreation. These three propositions about God's vision of work can be summed up in a single sentence and then examined in some detail.

Work, according to Catholic Christianity, is man's collaboration with God in the divine labor of natural and supernatural creation.[22] It was part of human destiny from the beginning. The mysterious opening pages of Genesis show Adam, still innocent, given charge of the plantation of Eden and told to cultivate it. It is only after his sin that work acquires those unhappy overtones of effort, toil, and fear of failure; work itself is not presented by the Bible as a penalty for sin. God is seen deliberately to have left His creation in an unfinished state and to have given mankind the vocation to develop it. The Divine Power that created oceans and continents, plants, birds, beasts, and men, could have directly created also the George Washington Bridge, great books and symphonies, paintings, houses, tools, and fabrics but chose instead to create all these indirectly through the labor of men. God, in short, made man an artist, a maker of things as He Himself is.

When men work, however, it is not only material creation that they develop but themselves as well. Think of what goes into the education and then the successful action of an artist, a plumber, a skilled mechanic, a chef, a surgeon, a good teacher or chemist, a sales manager, or an accountant. For these and many other kinds of work one must master intellectual skills and often also complex manual skills in which hand and mind are joined. Then, when a man works, these skills are expanded by intelligent exercise as the worker ponders, tests, and decides. A pioneer surveys the frontier wilderness. He dreams of what it can become, and after years of labor his dream takes body. The wilderness is transformed into rolling fields, gardens and wood plots, a house, and barns. The imprint of man's intelligence has humanized this patch of earth, and man himself has grown in wisdom and patience and courage as he labored.

Work does more than develop the earth and enlarge the worker's skills. It also contributes to his moral growth. Certain natural virtues, for instance, are needed by any good workman. He must have a decent respect for honest craftsmanship, and this is something which the manual worker learns more easily than the intellectual. A philosopher may be applauded initially for a theory full of errors if it is lit up by fireworks of erudition and rhetoric. But there is immediate criticism for the carpenter if his window frames warp in a month or the locksmith if the key does not work. Besides nurturing these dispositions of professional honesty and industry, work operates as a sort of extrinsic condition that is useful although not indispensable for removal of certain obstacles inhibiting the action of divine assistance. For one thing, the personality of the idler is poor soil for the expansion of the gift called grace. The lazy man has not the custom of taking life or himself seriously, and grace builds on what it finds. A person whose character has the solidity and equilibrium which sound work habits help to construct is more likely to respond to good impulses. Moreover, work very often confronts us with the need to make those significant moral decisions, those choices between good and evil or between good and less good, which so profoundly shape character.

Thus far in history, a great deal of work is streaked with boredom or strain and tempts us to laziness or selfishness. But when we resist these leanings and stick to a job despite its rigors because we know ourselves responsible not just for our own welfare but for that of others, then work itself becomes the occasion of moral advance. On the other hand, if the rewards of work tempt us to overabsorption in our occupations and the neglect of the contemplative dimension, or to ruthless struggle for riches and prestige, once again the moment of work is a moment of significant moral decision.

Finally, work develops, along with the earth and the worker, the material base of society and its spiritual center. It is plain that labor creates the whole physical framework of our communities—the homes, the roads, the bridges and railroads and airports, the sidewalks and sewers of towns. It runs the farms, factories, and offices that feed, shelter, govern, and maintain society. But more important than this, work can and should help develop that spirit of brotherhood without which community perishes. No doubt, this fails to happen often enough—ambition and rivalries at work can snuff this spirit out. But if it would be unrealistic to say that all work projects actually nourish fraternal feeling, people working in an office or factory, on a ship or in a store must fraternize, which is itself a first step toward fraternity.

What might be done, then, to provide an education for work that would consciously envision a total life with its rhythms of labor and leisure, action and contemplation, unified and interpreted by the Christian outlook? The promotion of such a humanism of work calls for a division of responsibility and must be the cooperative enterprise of several agencies.[23] For part of the task, the family is particularly qualified. Other aspects are more easily left to the school or to adult education programs, which often aim to complement or compensate. Those whose earlier schooling was largely bookish may want to try their hand literally at the making of useful or beautiful things, whereas those whose previous education was largely technical may prefer to turn as adults to literature or philosophy.

Since work, as we noted, not only supports life but matures personality, it has both an economic and a humanistic function; family and school will be chiefly concerned with the latter. We remarked in the second chapter that John Dewey effectively wove work activity into the program of elementary instruction because he thought it promoted problem-solving thinking and dispositions of responsibility and cooperativeness. He believed that the school's part in educating *through* work is best done when work experience is *re*-presented on a level different from the economic, being introduced precisely because it is a valuable human formation. Although parents cannot easily provide at home the academic education their children need, they can help them acquire an insight into the personal and social satisfactions of work as well as into its undeniable discipline. For instance, they can give children some experience of the joys of craftsmanship by supplying the simple tools and understanding guidance needed for easy carpentry or cooking projects in which the inspirations of work and play can be fused. This is more likely to happen if the older person works beside the younger and explains the process without prolonging it beyond the child's reasonable interest span or insisting on adult standards of technical competence. Of course, since there is no automatic connection even between interesting household chores and growth in wisdom and virtue, parents have to make those rudimentary tasks meaningful if their humanistic possibilities are to be exploited. But this they can hardly do unless they themselves relish the dignity of labor and find satisfaction in their own occupations.

Although the school, at least today, is the chief agency of systematic intellectual culture, it does not follow that work activities must fall completely outside its concern. The distinguished Thomist, Jacques Maritain, wrote: "There is no place closer to man than a workshop, and the intelligence of a man is not only in his head, but in his fingers too."[24] When he said this, Maritain was very much in the tradition of his master, for Aquinas had argued, in a little essay "On Manual Labor,"[25] that man's physical structure shows him to be naturally oriented toward work. The lower animals, said Thomas, find food within their reach and have furs and hides, teeth and claws, for covering and defense. But in place of these resources, men have two unique instruments: the hand and the mind. Thus they can take thought for their needs and devise and wield the tools, simple or complicated, to execute their designs.

Perhaps general schooling, although it is already heavily burdened, can contribute something here. For, of course, it is called on to introduce young people to the literary and historical, the scientific and mathematical, the philosophical and religious resources of our civilization. Schooling is also expected to furnish a certain amount of physical training, vocational guidance, and personal counseling, and to have some care for character growth. Might it also, somewhere along the line, prepare for wise occupational choice by adverting to the philosophical and theological concept of work as well as to the indices of aptitude? Then this moment of theory might be complemented by practical experience of the kind that shops and hobby clubs already often provide. When young craftsmen in a school workshop or in extracurricular activities set their own goals, plan their own strategy as far as feasible, and carry the project through as faithfully as they can, they discover the rewards and the price of making things *well*. They learn something about the potentialities of matter and something about their own human condition.

Christian educators would not require work projects to carry so large a share of character education as Dewey thought they could. Nor would they make social situations and conflicts the actual generators of moral rules rather than just a frequent occasion of their discovery. At the same time, they know that morally good action, which is most often an expression of altruism, is unfolded in the context of interpersonal relationships. It is quite true that work projects in the communities of home, school, parish, or

neighborhood can offer opportunities for young people to experience those values of fraternity, generosity, and cooperation which
are elsewhere taught rather abstractly. If they do acquire these
virtues, they are that much better prepared to turn their thought
and energy to that wider world scene, where the problems of
justice and peace loom so terrifyingly large.

THE GOOD SOCIETY

*In the social sphere, the Church has always wished to assume a
double function: first to enlighten minds in order to assist them to
discover the truth and find the right path to follow . . . and sec-
ondly to take part in action and to spread, with a real care for
service and effectiveness, the energies of the Gospel.*

Paul VI
Octogesima Adveniens[26]

Although mankind has the vocation and power to develop the
earth and to create civilizations, the Amish are not wrong in judging the results often equivocal. For instance, sometimes the power
itself is destructively exaggerated. In *The German Ideology* Marx
and Engels distinguished men from beasts precisely because of the
human capacity for work. More than a century later, a Chinese
woman composed some verses that were inscribed on a factory
wall:

The machine is my husband,
the factory is my family,
the fruits of my labor are my children.[27]

And it is quite possible, of course, to idolize work in practice without being a Marxist in theory.

Yet even if one's appreciation of work and its products is
properly balanced, one is bound to see that all civilizations are
deeply flawed. Imagine a middle-aged, reasonably well-informed
American Christian looking around him in the early 1970s. How
ambivalent he would find his world, and how unsure he would be
about the exact attitudes a Christian ought to take toward it. He
would disagree with those who say that American civilization is
so radically incompatible with the Gospel that all its fundamental
institutions must be opposed. For one thing, there is a strong
whiff of Utopianism about this appraisal, and we must be wary of
such a spirit, since it is apt to consent to cruelties in its doomed
effort to establish heaven on earth. Besides, many would find the
judgment unfair and say that even today American society partially

embodies the ideals of the Declaration of Independence. Indeed, Jean-François Revel argued that only in the United States can the political and economic freedom needed for constructive social change be found.[28]

Nevertheless, the anxious Christian is sadly troubled when he reflects on contemporary life in the United States, for there seem to be so many signs of bad times. There are the obvious break-downs in the web of our interconnected communities. The farming towns are fading away, and the decay of the cities has become a boring topic without ceasing to be an ominous reality. Meanwhile, the suburbs march into an ever denser thicket of problems. Generalizations about the moral climate are dangerous; there are, however, certain notable ambiguities. The movie *A Clockwork Orange* won an award as the best of 1971 from the bemused New York film critics. But one of the most distinguished of these re-viewers, Pauline Kael, tore that picture to pieces not so much for its eroticism as for what she called its pornography of brutality. Controls are equated with censorship in the pejorative sense; but as Miss Kael remarked, "when night after night atrocities are served up to us as entertainment, it's worth some anxiety."[29] Most people, at any rate, think it would be catastrophic if human relation-ships actually did reflect this degradation of sexuality and glori-fication of cruelty.

In fact, there is reason for worry about the state of Americans' relationships with one another in the national community. There is, for instance, the harsh inequity between the poor who go no-where and the middle class, exasperated at finding Portuguese rosé substituted for the champagne a Bermuda flight had promised. In 1954 the pastor of a southern parish was changed when he inte-grated the congregation on the Sunday following the Supreme Court's decision in the biracial public school cases. Since today he would be changed if he tried to impede integration, we can say that there is some progress. At the same time, prejudices acquire new styles among both whites and blacks. When someone men-tioned a proposal to build 25,000 units of low-income housing for blacks in Baltimore County, an official protested: "We don't even have enough for whites."[30] And as a subway train pulled out of the 42nd Street station in New York, a black youth leaned casually from a window to spit on a white man reading his paper on the platform.

If we turn from these disturbing images to consider the relation-ship of the United States and the other nations of the Atlantic com-munity to the so-called Third World, we are likely to feel even more uneasy. On the one hand, inconceivably vast sums, representing a disproportionate share of the federal budget, are spent on the defense establishment and its tragic adventures. On the other hand, there is the spectacle of the rich nations, in which most Christians live, monopolizing the earth's resources for a minority of the world's peoples. Paul VI voiced the Christian condemnation of this scandal in his 1967 encyclical, *Populorum Progressio:* "The poor nations remain ever poor while the rich ones become still richer. . . . We must repeat once more that the superfluous wealth of rich countries should be placed at the service of poor nations, the rule which up to now held good for the benefit of those nearest to us, must today be applied to all the needy of the world."

But it has not happened yet. For more than a generation before the Bishops' Synod of 1971, the single most eloquent Catholic voice calling for the rich nations to show justice toward the poor ones was that of Barbara Ward. Thus it was appropriate that on October 20, 1971, she keynoted the synod's discussion of world justice with a characteristically brilliant statement. She reminded the bishops that nearly a decade had passed since Vatican II had raised the issue. Yet the maldistribution of resources had grown steadily worse, and so had its evil effects. The third of humanity that has already crossed the threshold of the modern technological community continues, she pointed out, to control and consume at least 75 percent of these goods. Meanwhile, the wastes they produce pollute not only their own streams and airsheds but slop out into the oceans. She asked that the Church itself observe strict justice and poverty while it educated its members to the facts of injustice in the world and encouraged them to fight it. "Teach us, therefore, by word and example to love and respect this small planet which must carry all humanity, teach us to moderate our demands, share our resources and seek with all our brothers to make a reality of our prayer, 'Thy Kingdom Come.' "[31]

What will be required even for a modestly progressive realization of these aims? First of all, their acceptance. A philosophical argument can be constructed to show that the earth belongs to mankind as a whole, but the words may not be practically persuasive. Catholic Christians, however, were reminded by Vatican II that they "belong at one and the same time both to the People of God and to civil society."[32] Their faith, in turn, not only reinforces their civic obligations but imposes much more sweeping demands of charity and justice. Every thoughtful Christian knows that the command to love God is chiefly fulfilled by loving and serving other people, although the practical implications may be rather differently understood. The Catholic emphasis, for example, is not that of the great Karl Barth who in 1948 told an Assembly of the World Council of Churches:

We ought to give up every thought that the care of the Church, the care of the world is *our* care. . . . We are not the ones to change this evil world into a good one. . . . By God's design is not meant something like a Christian Marshall plan. . . . All that is required of us is that in the midst of the political and social disorder of the world we should be His witnesses, as disciples and servants of Jesus.[33]

No doubt, all Christians must confess that the consummation of His Kingdom will be brought about by God alone. Moreover, since American Catholics as a group have been inclined toward that intense patriotism which can too easily decline into the vice of nationalism, they need to meditate on the warning with which Werner Stark concluded the third volume of his study, *The Sociology of Religion.* Two essential features of a Universal Church, he wrote, are its noninvolvement in any particular class structure and its noninvolvement in any particular national interest. But identification with social class or nation is one thing; working to heal social disorders, which are often enough the products of inequities among groups or countries, is another.[34] Catholics, like many other Christians, believe that it is discipleship itself which requires service in the effort to embody somewhat the Gospel ideals in all human communities.

It is easy to make this general statement; hard to reduce it to a practical blueprint, and even harder to live it. Certain British public figures seem able to speak to this point with a directness unmatched by their American counterparts. For example, Michael Stewart, who became Foreign Secretary in the Labor Government in 1968, once wrote to the *Times Educational Supplement* to say: "Christians . . . believe that our capacity to enjoy eternal life depends on how we perform our duty here; and that part of that duty, especially for those concerned in public affairs, is to try to make human institutions more just." But this ideal, which is again that of a synthesis, is difficult indeed, as Enoch Powell strikingly testified in a remarkable dialogue with Malcolm Muggeridge in the London church of St. Mary-le-Bow. His words revealed a spirit far more subtle and sensitive than his notorious racial doctrines would have suggested. He did not admit, to be sure, that these doctrines were un-Christian, but he did show that he was poignantly aware of what he called Christianity's impossible demands. As a politician he thought he had to lead a "life which does not fulfill the absolute commandments . . . placed upon us by Christ and the Church," although he hoped that a politician's Christian faith would make some difference in his public life. But the demands of Christianity, he thought, had been made deliberately impracticable by its Founder. "Indeed, the religious duty is 100 percent. I find this over and over again asserted by Christ and misheard—because it is so painful to hear—by us."[35]

What then are these impossible demands? They are to make real the Christian ideal of community. And as Max Scheler remarked, this ideal cannot be abandoned simply because we have thus far failed to make it a reality. Realizing the ideal requires first that Christians form their conscience about existing social conditions, and second that they *act* in cooperation with all honest men for the betterment of societies. Both these phases are beset with pitfalls, particularly for those exercising ministries or special offices in the Church. For when bishops, priests, brothers, and nuns speak and act, or fail to do so, the whole Church appears peculiarly implicated and is blamed for failures and imbalances.

At the 1971 synod, for example, the bishops ranged pointedly over a wide variety of issues: the evils of racism and colonialism; the population and ecological problems; restrictions on political freedom; the evils of stockpiling armaments—it was the American Cardinal John Krol whose intervention indicted that particular injustice—and authoritarian regimes' torture of their opponents. The synod document on "Justice in the World" echoed Barbara Ward's emphasis on educating Catholics to a knowledge of these worldwide injustices and inspiring them to work to eliminate such wrongs. At present, it said, education often actually encourages a narrow individualism, although it should "awaken a critical sense, which will lead us to reflect on the society in which we live and on its values . . . [and] make men ready to renounce these values when they cease to promote justice for all men."[36]

But the bishops explicitly declined to provide programs of detailed action, and a cranky Italian journalist complained in Milan's *Corriere della Serra* that the synod had failed fully to resolve the problems "of the Church's active presence in the world."[37] Yet it was unreasonable to have expected that it would. In fact, some critics thought it had tried to be too specific, whereas others thought it should have skipped all pronouncement and focused simply on the need for action.

No doubt it is action that matters most. We noted earlier that the Gospel itself insists on belief issuing in action. These pages, however, are not the place for detailing programs for social improvements, even if the writer were competent to do so—which he is not. However, certain guidelines for the evolution of such programs can be drawn from the documents of Vatican II, the social statements of John XXIII and Paul VI, and that synod paper on world justice. We shall simply list these and refrain entirely from wispy applications, which would only disgust men and women who have had practical experience. One such person has written:

Let me put it simply and with more than a trace of arrogance. I am tired of reading and listening to stuff by people who have never been there: about unions and labor relations, about politics and public service, about under-developed countries and foreign aid, about poverty and the black ghetto, about the slow and painful process by which the powerless attain power and self-respect. I have been there, all those places, not just to visit but to live and work. By and large, it's not the way they say it is.[38]

From the beginning, Christians have known that they must help one another if they are to be disciples of the Master, Who said He was among them as one who serves. Vatican II's "Decree on the Missionary Activity of the Church" recognized that men and women ordinarily witness to Christ "by their life and works in the home, in their social group, and in their own professional circle." The synod echoed this when it noted realistically that "Christians' specific contribution to justice is the day-to-day life of the individual believer acting like the leaven of the Gospel in his family, his school, his work and his social and civic life."[39]

Nevertheless, four rather new specifications of the second commandment can be distilled from these documents. There is first of all the planetary accent, as it has come to be called. A contemporary Christian may spend his life in a village, but his vision and concern must embrace the world. In our times, said the council, "a special obligation binds us to make ourselves the neighbor of absolutely every person."[40] It is now easier than ever before to appreciate the oneness of the human race and to see that the Church should, if it is to be true to its nature, exercise a responsibility for all mankind. Christians must be, as Cardinal Marty remarked at the synod, men of the universal community. Second, service of others is not to be left to the action of individual Catholics; it must also be expressed through the collective efforts of the worldwide Church, as well as by the local churches and those forms of organized action whose development the council encouraged. In the third place, it is recognized that laymen, in addition to sharing the mission of spreading the Gospel, are those chiefly responsible for transforming social institutions. They are to be the stewards of Christian wisdom, said the council; it is up to them "to be a leaven animating temporal affairs from within, disposing them always to become as Christ would wish them."[41] Finally, this whole work is to be carried on not as a Christian monopoly but in collaboration with all men of good will.

And what are the goals of this collaboration? Chiefly two: a more equitable distribution of the world's resources among all people, and a securing of peace among nations. These, in turn, are means serving two dominant human purposes. The poor simply lack the economic base required for that personal appropriation of culture and that true exercise of freedom which are the chief constituents of the humanistic development sought by Catholicism for all men and women. Catholics must therefore work to help create a social order in which all individuals can better arrive at the dignity of personhood by developing their native gifts and experiencing that religious conversion which divine grace effects.[42] In the second place, these benefits of justice and peace promote that unity and solidarity of the entire human family which Christianity sees as the goal of this world's history.

Of all the aims of education, none is so difficult as bringing people to accept and serve these social purposes. This is because the price is so high and the countervailing force so great. For the cost is self-denial and the opposition comes from that profound egoism which is the root of sin. The basic evil, said Camus in *The Fall,* is that men cannot even once forget themselves for someone else. Is this true? Some things can be said, in any case. To begin with, if the conservationists are to be believed, cutbacks in consumption will soon be unavoidable if the natural environment is to endure. Nations might discover something like brotherhood in the common need to survive.

In any case, the crisis itself serves to underscore an essential Christian teaching which we have not yet emphasized. This is the Lord's unqualified insistence on renunciation as a condition of discipleship: "Anyone who loves his life loses it." A certain moderation of self-aggrandizement is essential for Christians, no matter what the social conditions. But to practice collective moderation in the sharing of the world's wealth will require overcoming not only individual but group selfishness. Since this egoism can only be displaced by altruism, we shall have to love those with whom we share the earth. But is it not impossible to love billions of others whom we have never seen and whose numbers we can scarcely conceive?

Teilhard de Chardin, who was keenly conscious of this difficulty, formulated afresh the Christian response to it. This answer reminds us that although we may not be able to love multitudes, we can love God, the superpersonal center of existence. God, however, does indeed love each one of this unimaginable throng. By being united to this Divine Center, therefore, men are in some mysterious way united to one another. Within the Church itself there are evidences that this unity is not a mirage, that despite all the sins and failures, a great many disparate people have shared this community and have sustained life and hope on that account. Years ago that unusual thinker, Randolph Bourne, wrote that the Catholic Church "saves men as members of the Beloved Community, and not as individuals . . . When one is saved by Catholicism, one becomes a democrat."[43] There is enough truth here to encourage us to take the Church as a pledge that mankind may yet by God's favor become a Beloved Community.

POSTSCRIPT ON THE SCHOOL

. . . the Catholic School retains its immense importance in the circumstances of our times too.

Vatican II
"Declaration on Christian Education," n. 8

Early in March 1969 former British Prime Minister Harold Macmillan was opening an extension built for the 300-year-old Archbishop Tenison's Church of England Grammar School in Kennington. In doing so he observed: "I hope we shall fight to the bitter end for church schools. They mean something more than the teaching of scripture or the Bible." For in these schools, he said, children can be educated in an atmosphere "which has something precious in it, in which they can absorb, consciously or unconsciously, the traditions of Christian life and religion."[44] In this there was some echo of François Mauriac's recollection of the Catholic school he had attended in Bordeaux about 1905. That school provided no real religious education, Mauriac thought later, but it shaped a Catholic sensibility, if not a Catholic way of thinking.[45]

In the United States, as Catholic schools advanced into the 1970s they were surely aiming to provide a sound religious education along with secular culture and to develop Catholic intelligence as well as sensibility.[46] Nonetheless, they no longer seemed quite so sure of their purposes as they had once been and their existence was threatened by hard economic facts. Moreover, not all American Catholics were of Mr. Macmillan's mind, and the schools were also being questioned in theory. Given this uneasiness, we might wonder why this book has so little to say about the Catholic school itself. There are two reasons. The church school is ultimately a means for achieving the purposes of Christian education, but it is not absolutely indispensable. These pages, however, have been limited to an effort at identifying what Catholicism necessarily requires of education always and everywhere. This limitation can be accepted with less regret, since there are already available books that describe and effectively make the case for the American Catholic school system.[47]

The few comments to be made here are projected at a high level of generality and have particularly in mind the elementary and the secondary school. This is partly because these are the schools whose existence is most questioned and partly because, as Dewey once said about his own concentration on childhood education, the quality of the foundation determines the soundness of the whole structure. Still, just because these observations are so general they are often applicable also to higher education.

In the 1970s three kinds of objections were being lodged, though not for the first time, against the idea of the American Catholic school. The most formidable of these was economic. At the 1952 convention of the National Education Association, Agnes E. Meyer, an unyielding opponent of parochial schools, suggested that if governmental aid were strictly withheld from these institutions, the Catholic people would eventually be forced by their unbearable financial weight to give them up. Twenty years later it appeared that Mrs. Meyer's cheerful prediction might well come true. The schools by then were actually receiving various kinds of supplementary governmental aid, but not for the steadily rising substantial costs of instruction and buildings. At the same time, vocations to the teaching sisterhoods and brotherhoods had sharply declined while expenditures for lay teachers' salaries and for such improvements as smaller class sizes skyrocketed. Beginning in 1963, therefore, each year saw hundreds of schools closing or consolidating and enrollments decreasing annually by close to 7 percent in the elementary schools and 4 percent in the high schools.

Even before these fiscal crises blew in, the schools had been criticized for serving only a portion of the Catholic population, since they had never enrolled much more than half the children of elementary school age and about a third of those of high school age. Critics argued, therefore, that the manpower and money of parishes and dioceses ought to be invested instead in programs serving not only all the Catholic children but Catholics of all ages. Finally, the schools' performance was sometimes indicted. Before any systematic large-scale studies had been made, it used to be hinted darkly that these schools were academically inferior. The charges were usually pointed up by grim anecdotes about insensitive or clownish teachers, authoritarian methods, and the practices of a naïve pietism. In the 1960s, however, a number of solid studies finally were made, and they showed that students of the Catholic schools performed as a whole above average when measured by national test norms or by such indicators as percentages going on to college. As a writer commenting on materials gathered for the work of New York State's Fleischmann Commission put it: the Catholic schools "accomplish their educational aim whereas the urban public schools do not . . . Catholic schools are better than public schools . . . [and] are especially good in the cities."[48]

After the first of these studies appeared, certain Catholic critics of the schools shifted their ground. Academic achievements are all very well, they said, but since the schools are much less effective in religious education than they are in achieving secular aims, why have them at all? Or why not abolish Catholic schools as presently constituted and replace them by a few good but quite secular institutions run by Catholics and open to all comers.

These objections are noted in deference to realism. Some are formidable enough, others questionable. For instance, it is surely much harder to measure religious commitment than mathematical ability and, therefore, more risky to appraise the schools' success in religious education. In any case, none of the critiques is irresistible and solid rebuttals exist. Particularly useful is Michael O'Neill's *New Schools in a New Church* (cited in Note 47). But even if these objections were more intractable than they are, they would not invalidate the rationale for the Catholic schools, except insofar as the difficulties of attaining any ideal may always be reckoned arguments against it.

That rationale has several components. We might recall that Christian faith summons men and women to a union with the Lord which is profoundly interior and to a communion with one another in the religious society. Therefore, membership in this Church is quite indispensable for Catholics, since it constitutes that fellowship and creates the ordinary context for growing into that union with Christ. Today, however, people belong to churches because they have chosen to do so. They are no longer dropped into them by birth or retained there by social convention. It is more than ever true, as Charles Williams said, that the Church must begin the labor of regenerating mankind all over again with each new generation. It is within the family and parish that this process begins; but those communities are usually unable to complete it any more than the daily round of life in home and neighborhood can fully educate for adult citizenship apart from schools. If the Catholic school is reasonably effective, it will do what neither family nor parish can do, and this precisely because it is both a school and Christian.

Because it is a school it provides academic instruction at least as competently as the public institution down the block and so it serves the needs of civil society and deserves its support. Because it is Christian it tries to develop religious maturity along with the other aspects of personal growth and to harmonize all these zones with one another. Christians, as we have said often enough, must synthesize the Gospel and human culture in their persons and in their action; and the church school is the chief institution proposing systematically to help them do so.

This requires that the Catholic school honor in practice and in theory Christianity's twofold character of a teaching and a way-of-life. Consider the importance of the very fact that this school provides religious education along with other studies and opportunities for worship along with other nonacademic activities. For this program is a concrete recognition of the relevance and dignity of the religious dimension of life, which reinforces the values embodied by parents who are serious Christians (although it may not overcome the influence of parents who are religiously indifferent). After all, parents who cherish music and the other arts do not want their children to spend hours in a philistine school which ignores these noblest of natural achievements and perhaps clumsily insists that only the sciences properly illumine experience. It was a kindred conviction which Cardinal Heenan of Westminster expressed when putting the case for the Catholic school: "Any sacrifice is thought worthwhile which spares children the strain of being taught one set of spiritual values at home and another at school."[49]

Those values, like the synthesis, must be taught and not left to children to puzzle out by themselves. They are taught, to be sure, in several ways: in deed as well as in word; by example as well as by precept. This means that, within its limits, the Christian school must be a community in which the Christian doctrine is better communicated because the Christian way is embodied there to some degree. Given the present methods of financing them, it would be unfair to expect American Catholic schools to be as well-equipped as the most affluent public ones. It is fair, though, to expect their atmosphere to be distinctively humane and their teachers outstanding for kindness and dedication.

In practice, church schools sometimes have these endowments and sometimes they do not, the second case being a sad betrayal of their essence. For even when the Christian school simply reflects the questionable educational practices of its locale and is no worse than its secular colleagues, the point is that it should be better. An East African recollecting his days in a Catholic Mission school said that each Monday the priest-headmaster caned the boys who had missed Mass the day before.[50] That school was in an area where British traditions prevailed and punishment of this sort was standard. But we must still ask if a Catholic school should not be expected to rise above such traditions.

We know that the ideal is possible because at least on occasion Catholic schools transcend contemporary custom. In the South and in the District of Columbia, where segregation was imposed by law, the Catholic schools were also once segregated out of deference to bad custom. But the archdioceses of St. Louis and Washington did integrate their parochial schools well ahead of the *Brown* decision. In the late 1960s the press reported from cities like Bogotá and Buenos Aires that wealthy, conservative parents were incensed because the convent schools were introducing their daughters to the countries' social problems. Critical discussion of these issues became a metaphor for new curricula, much as the study of French and flower arrangement had been symbols for the old. "The school," said one Argentinian father, "was upsetting my whole household."[51] A youth in Spanish Harlem told an interviewer some years ago:

When I reached sixth grade, I couldn't read. The teachers, most of them, didn't give a damn. But when I was in seventh grade, I went to a Catholic school for a year. They put a kind of wrench in my mind and opened it a crack and I began to see that there was a world outside my block. Man, that school cared, about me and about everybody, and they wanted to teach and they wanted me to learn.[52]

That says enough and says it well. The theory of Christian education is built with materials from many sources, including the precious constituents derived from the Gospel. Those evangelical principles are simple, not in the sense of easy, but open rather than secret. John XXIII had a gift of making this clear. Some sentences from his Last Testament reflect that Gospel which should animate Christian schools and so we may end with them here:

Love one another, my dear children.
Seek rather what unites, not what may separate you from one another.
As I take leave, or better still, as I say "Till we meet again,"
Let me remind you of the important things in life:
  Our Blessed Saviour Jesus,
  His Good News,
  His Holy Church,
  Truth and Kindness.

NOTES

1. Quoted in *The Tablet,* 224 (June 13, 1970), 578.

2. The Synod, which met in Rome from September 30 to November 6, 1971, is not to be confused with a General Council which brings together all the Catholic Bishops to speak to the entire Church. The synod was rather a gathering of some 200 bishops (along with a few nonepiscopal others) who represented the various national hierarchies of the world. It discussed two topics of wide interest, the ministerial priesthood and world justice; but its final statements on these matters were directly addressed to Paul VI, whom the synod was understood to be advising. The synod got rather an unfavorable press and no doubt had its share of the procedural difficulties that afflict all group deliberations. But its document on "Justice in the World," from which we shall draw, is very valuable, and the discussions of it which were summarized each week in the English edition of *L'Osservatore Romano* were highly instructive.

3. "Pastoral Constitution on the Church in the Modern World," quoted in the English translation of *The Documents of Vatican II,* Walter M. Abbott, S.J., gen. ed. (New York: Guild-America-Association Presses, 1966), n. 77, p. 289.

4. From a sermon of June 2, 1839, "Unreal Words," quoted from *Cardinal Newman's Best Plain Sermons,* Vincent Ferrer Blehl, S.J., ed. (New York: Herder and Herder, 1964), p. 79.

5. The remarks quoted are from two stories on the Amish in the *New York Times:* February 16, 1971, p. 35, under the byline of Donald Janson; November 28, 1965, p. 85, under the byline of Walter Rugaber.

6. Tertullian (c. 160–230), *Apology,* c. 41, *Educational Ideals in the Ancient World,* trans. William Barclay (London: Collins, 1959), p. 194.

7. Tertullian, *De Praescriptionibus Haereticorum,* vii. 9–13, trans. S. L. Greenslade, *Early Latin Theology,* Vol. V, *The Library of Christian Classics* (London: SCM Press, 1956), p. 36.

8. These are taken from three of the Anglican sermons, *Cardinal Newman's Best Plain Sermons, op. cit.,* pp. 12, 42, 170–171.

9. Leo XIII, *Rerum Novarum* quoted from the translation, "Rights and Duties of Capital and Labor," in *The Church Speaks to the Modern World: The Social Teachings of Leo XIII,* Etienne Gilson, ed. (Garden City, N.Y.: Doubleday, 1954), p. 216.

10. Leo XIII, *Immortale Dei* ("On the Christian Constitution of States"), in *The Church Speaks to the Modern World, op. cit.,* p. 179.

11. Pius XI, in "Apostolic Constitution on Universities and Faculties of Ecclesiastical Studies" (*Deus Scientiarum Dominus*), 1931. The text is in the Vatican publication, *Acta Apostolicae Sedis,* 23 (July 1931), 241.

12. Pius XI, Encyclical on "Christian Education of Youth" (often referred

to in the customary fashion by its opening words as *Divini Illius Magistri*), cited from *The Catholic Mind,* 28 (February 1903), 63.

13. Pius XII, "Christmas Eve Address: 1953," quoted from the translation in *The Catholic Mind,* 52 (March 1954), 175–176.
14. Pius XII, "To the Union of Italian Teachers," text of an address, September 4, 1949, *The Catholic Mind,* 48 (September 1950), 572.
15. See *The Documents of Vatican II, op. cit.,* p. 315.
16. "Pastoral Constitution on the Church in the Modern World," *The Documents of Vatican II, op. cit.,* n. 36, p. 233.
17. These themes of *now* and *not yet* are so central in the New Testament that scholars working from a variety of angles point them out. See, for instance, Alan Richardson, *An Introduction to the Theology of the New Testament* (New York: Harper & Row, 1958), p. 89 and Edwyn Bevan, *Symbolism and Belief* (New York: Macmillan, 1938), p. 117, n. 1. For a meditation on this whole notion of the combination of opposites, see a tiny book that remains one of the best summaries of the spirit of Catholicism: Peter Lippert, S.J., *The Essence of the Catholic* (New York: Kenedy, 1930). This is an anonymous translation of three lectures delivered at Heidelberg in 1922.
18. "Pastoral Constitution on the Church in the Modern World," *The Documents of Vatican II, op. cit.,* n. 36, p. 233.
19. Saint Thomas Aquinas, *Summa Theologiae,* IIa–IIae, q. 145, a. 1, ad 1, in *St. Thomas Aquinas: Philosophical Texts,* trans. Thomas Gilby (London: Oxford, 1951), p. 301.
20. John XXIII, Encyclical Letter of May 15, 1961, *Mater et Magistra,* cited from an American edition: (New York: American Press, 1961), n. 246, p. 65.
21. Much of the material on work here is adapted from the writer's earlier book, *Work and Education* (Chicago: Loyola University Press, 1959), particularly Chapters 1, 5, and 6.
22. In the "Pastoral Constitution on the Church in the Modern World," Vatican II said: "For when, by the work of his hands or with the aid of technology, man develops the earth so that it can bear fruit and become a dwelling worthy of the whole human family, and when he consciously takes part in the life of social groups, he carries out the design of God. Manifested at the beginning of time, the divine plan is that man should subdue the earth, bring creation to perfection, and develop himself. When a man so acts he simultaneously obeys the great Christian commandment that he place himself at the service of his brother men." *Documents of Vatican II, op. cit.,* n. 57, p. 262. The sentence that immediately follows this passage is a tribute to intellectual work in the arts and sciences; no. 67, p. 275 formulates the concept of work as a partnership with God in bringing material and spiritual creation to perfection.

23. John W. Donohue, S.J., *Work and Education, op. cit.,* pp. 195 ff.

24. Jacques Maritain, *Education at the Crossroads* (New Haven: Yale University Press, 1943), p. 45.

25. Saint Thomas Aquinas, *De Opere Manuali, Quodlibet* VII, a. 17, c. Articles 17 and 18 of *Quodlibet* VII constitute the *Quaestio disputata de opere manuali.* A modern edition is to be had in R. P. Mandonnet, ed., *S. Thomae Aquinatis questiones quodlibetales* (Paris: P. Lethielleux, 1926), pp. 289–296.

26. Paul VI, *Octogesima Adveniens* ("On the Occasion of the Eightieth Anniversary of the Encyclical *Rerum Novarum*"), Apostolic Letter sent to Cardinal Maurice Roy, as President of the Council of the Laity and of the Pontifical Commission on Justice and Peace, on May 14, 1971. The text quoted is from the edition published by the United States Catholic Conference (Washington, D.C.: 1971), n. 48, p. 28.

27. Quoted by Bernard Ullmann, "China's Grim Winter: A Reporter's Notebook," *New York Times Magazine,* February 19, 1961, p. 5.

28. A Polish woman emigrated to New York with her husband and wrote six years later: "Among some of our American-born friends it is not fashionable to be enthusiastic about America. There is Vietnam, drugs, urban and racial conflicts, poverty and pollution. Undoubtedly, this country faces urgent and serious problems. But what we, the newcomers, see are not only the problems but also democratic solutions being sought and applied . . . we are also in love with America. Standing in the street, amidst the noise and pollution, we suddenly realize what luck and joy it is to live in a free country." Janina Atkins, "God Bless America!" *New York Times,* November 26, 1970, p. 31.

29. Pauline Kael, "The Current Cinema: Stanley Strangelove," *The New Yorker,* 47 (January 1, 1972), 50–53.

30. *New York Times,* June 3, 1971, p. 26. This article, under the byline of Linda Greenhouse, is one of a series of five "on the growth, complexities and attitudes of suburban America."

31. Quoted from the text of Barbara Ward's "Intervention" as reported, apparently with some abridgment or paraphrasing in *L'Osservatore Romano,* weekly English edition, November 18, 1971, p. 7.

32. "Decree on the Missionary Activity of the Church," *Documents of Vatican II, op. cit.,* n. 21, p. 611.

33. As reported in *Time,* 52 (September 13, 1948), 55.

34. Werner Stark, *The Sociology of Religion: A Study of Christendom,* Vol. III: *The Universal Church* (New York: Fordham University Press, 1967), p. 438.

35. See *The Times Educational Supplement,* January 3, 1964, p. 15, and "Christianity's Impossible Demands—An Exchange between Malcolm Muggeridge and Enoch Powell in the Cheapside Church of St. Mary-le-Bow," *The Listener,* 85 (January 14, 1971), 51–53.

36. The text of the synod's document, "Justice in the World" is quoted from *L'Osservatore Romano,* weekly English edition, December 16, 1971, pp. 5–7. For a good brief account of the synod's work on this topic see Arthur McCormack, "The Synod and World Justice," *The Tablet* (November 20, 1971), 1115.

37. Quoted from *The Tablet,* 225 (November 20, 1971), 1129.

38. John C. Cort, "The Evolution of a Catholic Worker," *Commonweal,* 93 (January 8, 1971), 346.

39. See "Decree on the Missionary Activity of the Church," *The Documents of Vatican II, op. cit.,* n. 21, p. 611, and the text of the synod statement as given in *L'Osservatore Romano,* weekly English edition, December 16, 1971, p. 6.

40. "Pastoral Constitution on the Church in the Modern World," *The Documents of Vatican II, op. cit.,* n. 27, p. 226.

41. "Decree on the Apostolate of the Laity," *The Documents of Vatican II, op. cit.,* n. 14, p. 505, and "Decree on the Missionary Activity of the Church," *ibid.,* n. 15, p. 603.

42. In an admirable little book Oscar Cullmann argued that Christ was neither a revolutionary nor a defender of the existing order. His "eschatological realism" made Him stress individual change of character and not social reform. However, as Cullmann observed, Christians came to see that the end of the world was not as imminent as had once been thought. "But as soon as centuries are reckoned with, it must necessarily be acknowledged that more just social structures also promote the individual change of character required by Jesus. A reciprocal action is therefore required between the conversion of the individual and the reform of structures, even though the former must remain the principal factor in the life of the Christian." *Jesus and the Revolutionaries,* trans. Gareth Putnam (New York: Harper & Row, 1970), p. 55.

43. From the essay, "This Older Generation," in Randolph Bourne, *The History of a Literary Radical and Other Papers,* introduction by Van Wyck Brooks (New York: S. A. Russell, 1956), p. 303.

44. Quoted in *The Times Educational Supplement,* March 14, 1969, p. 829.

45. Quoted from an essay by the German Catholic novelist Heinrich Böll in *The Times Literary Supplement,* September 28, 1964, p. 884.

46. See, for instance, the impressive materials prepared by James J. DiGiacomo, S.J., for religious education in high schools under the general heading *Conscience and Concern* (New York: Holt, Rinehart & Winston, 1969). A series of attractive booklets provides readings and guides for reflection and discussion of current religious and social issues: Conscience and Authority, Violence, Race, Church Involvement, Faith, Sexuality, Meaning, and Church Membership. And this is but

one illustration of the creative ferment in the field of religious education.

47. See especially, for discussion of the parochial schools, Michael O'Neill, *New Schools in a New Church: Toward a Modern Philosophy of Catholic Education* (Collegeville, Minn.: Saint John's University Press, 1971), and Neil G. McClusky, S.J., *Catholic Viewpoint in Education,* rev. ed. (Garden City, N.Y.: Doubleday Image Books, 1962). Father O'Neill provides instructive comment on the implications of the two chief large-scale studies of Catholic elementary and secondary schools, *viz.,* Andrew M. Greeley and Peter H. Rossi, *The Education of Catholic Americans* (Chicago: Aldine, 1966), and the report of the Carnegie-sponsored Notre Dame study edited by Reginald A. Neuwien, *Catholic Schools in Action: The Notre Dame Study of Catholic Elementary and Secondary Schools in the United States* (Notre Dame, Ind.: University of Notre Dame Press, 1966). John Courtney Murray, S.J., discussed the issues of government aid for these schools in *We Hold These Truths; Catholic Reflections on the American Proposition* (New York: Sheed and Ward, 1960), pp. 143–154. On Catholic higher education, see the several studies of Andrew M. Greeley, particularly: *Religion and Career: A Study of College Graduates* (New York: Sheed and Ward, 1963); *The Changing Catholic College* (Chicago: Aldine, 1967), and *From Backwater to Mainstream: A Profile of Catholic Higher Education* (New York: McGraw-Hill, 1969). This last work has an interesting concluding "Commentary" by David Riesman. Also consult Christopher Jencks and David Riesman, "The Catholics and Their Colleges," *The Public Interest,* n. 7 (Spring 1967), 79–101, and n. 8 (Summer 1967), 49–74. Other worthwhile books on this topic are Robert Hassenger, ed., *The Shape of Catholic Higher Education* (Chicago: University of Chicago Press, 1967), and Manning M. Patillo, Jr., and Donald M. Mackenzie, *Church-Sponsored Higher Education in the United States: Report of the Danforth Commission* (Washington, D.C.: American Council on Education, 1966). Many of these books also have useful bibliographies.

48. Maurice R. Berube, "Is This School Necessary?" *Commonweal,* 95 (January 14, 1972), 342.

49. John Carmel Cardinal Heenan, "Basis for a Christian Life," *The Times Educational Supplement,* April 4, 1969, p. 1105.

50. J. Mutuku Nzioki, "Thorns in the Grass: The Story of a Kamba Boy," in Lorene K. Fox, ed., *East African Childhood: Three Versions* (Nairobi: Oxford University Press, 1967), p. 112.

51. *New York Times,* January 14, 1968, p. 23, and May 4, 1969, p. 27.

52. Richard Hammer, "Report from a Spanish Harlem 'Fortress,'" *New York Times Magazine,* January 5, 1964, p. 37.

Index

73 74 75 76 77 9 8 7 6 5 4 3 2 1